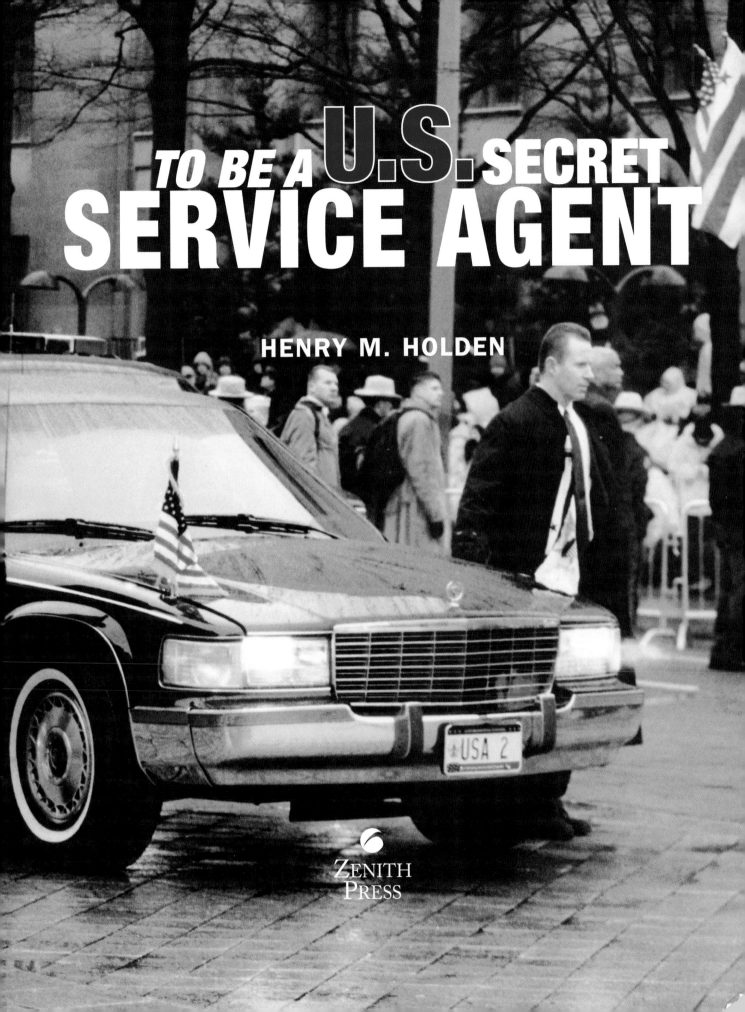

TO BE A U.S. SECRET SERVICE AGENT

HENRY M. HOLDEN

ZENITH PRESS

First published in 2006 by Zenith Press, an imprint of MBI Publishing Company, Galtier Plaza, Suite 200, 380 Jackson Street, St. Paul, MN 55101-3885 USA

MBI Publishing Company titles are also available at discounts in bulk quantity for industrial or sales-promotional use. For details write to Special Sales Manager at MBI Publishing Company, Galtier Plaza, Suite 200, 380 Jackson Street, St. Paul, MN 55101-3885 USA

ISBN-13: 978-0-7603-2293-2
ISBN-10: 0-7603-2293-7

Editors: Steve Gansen and Lindsay Hitch
Designer: Kally Lane

Unless otherwise noted, all photographs are courtesy of the United States Secret Service.

Printed in China

On the front cover:
The presidential motorcade progresses down Pennsylvania Avenue during the presidential inaugural parade. *Department of Defense*

On the frontispiece:
The motto of the United States Secret Service is, "Worthy of Trust and Confidence."

On the title page:
A parade limousine at the 2001 presidential inauguration. The license plate "USA 2" indicates it is the vice president's limousine. That plate is only used during inauguration ceremonies. All other times the parade limousines carry generic Washington, D.C., plates.

On the contents page:
This Special Agent is examining documents that may be evidence in a crime. Any potential evidence must not be contaminated by fingerprints.

On the back cover (*Clockwise from left*):
One team is designated to relocate the protectee and others are assigned to meet and neutralize the threat.

Motorcade Support Unit (MSU) provides skilled motorcycle tactical support during motorcade movements for the president, vice president, and other protectees when they travel in Washington, D.C. This includes escort, traffic control, and safe, unhindered transportation for protectees.

President-elect Dwight D. Eisenhower is accompanied by outgoing President Harry S. Truman on the way to Eisenhower's inauguration. Presidential security in 1952 appears to be two agents (in hats) behind the open-top car. Looking back at Truman is Senator Hubert H. Humphrey, who later became President Lyndon Johnson's vice president. *Library of Congress*

About the Author
Henry M. Holden is the author of 13 adult books, including MBI's *To Be A U.S. Air Force Pilot* and *To Be An FBI Special Agent*, 19 children's books, and more than 600 magazine articles on aviation history. In 1994, he received the New Jersey Institute of Technology Author's Award, and that same year Holden was mentioned in the Congressional Record for his works on women in aviation. Holden has been an aviation commentator for the History Channel and lives in northwestern New Jersey.

CONTENTS

Preface

While I was researching and writing this book, I witnessed firsthand some of the challenges the Secret Service willingly accepts and admirably succeeds in accomplishing. On June 14, 2004, former President Ronald Reagan passed away. The Secret Service had not had a state funeral in over thirty years, and any personnel who were part of that team had retired long before. The three-day funeral, with some of the tightest security ever implemented, went off flawlessly.

During the summer of 2004, the Secret Service was faced with the Democratic and Republican National Conventions. Both huge security concerns, the conventions ended successfully, without security incidents.

On January 18, 2005, a man threatened to blow up his van near the White House unless his son-in-law was released from jail. He was taken into custody before he could set off the bottles of gasoline in the van.

Two days later, the presidential inauguration and parade, the largest security challenge in the 140-year history of the Secret Service, was accomplished without a single security issue.

An airspace intrusion alarm put the White House on alert on April 27, 2005. Secret Service agents rushed the president from the Oval Office into an underground shelter. The warning was later revealed to have been a false alarm due to a technical problem.

On May 10, 2005, President Bush was giving a speech in Tbilisi, the capital of the Republic of Georgia, when a man tossed a device later identified as an unexploded grenade within 100 feet of the stage where the president was standing. Two months later, a man accused of throwing the live grenade was shot in a gunfight with local police. According to CNN, the Secret Service said, "We were not involved" in the incident but "we continue to monitor the Georgian investigation."

The day after the grenade incident, a private plane flew into Washington, D.C., restricted airspace and allegedly within three miles of the White House, forcing evacuation of the building. The president was out bike riding at the time.

On June 30, 2005, another private pilot broke the no-fly zone over Washington, D.C., and the White House staff was within minutes of being relocated. A week later, on July 7, a private plane flew into restricted airspace over Camp David, Maryland. The Secret Service would not say if the president was there.

Today's Secret Service personnel are an ordinary group of people doing an extraordinary job, an honor few Americans experience. They believe in what they do and know why they are doing it. For most, it is not just a job, but also a way of life, and about doing the right thing. They will continue to uphold the tradition of being "worthy of trust and confidence" and mark it a good day when nothing bad happens to anybody they are sworn to protect.

Acknowledgments

To Be a U.S. Secret Service Agent is the result, in part, of the willingness of the Secret Service to allow this writer access to its agents and training facilities. This book would not have been possible, or as informative, without the Secret Service's cooperation and trust that it would be an honest portrayal of the training that young men and women undergo to become Special Agents and uniformed officers.

Since the individuals who contributed are part of the larger team, they have asked that I not acknowledge anyone individually as contributing to this effort. You know who you are, and you have my sincere thanks. I wish to thank each of the professionals anonymously quoted in this book. You have given me a greater appreciation for the valuable work you do.

A special thanks to Steve Gansen, my editor, for being professional, helpful, and always generous with his time. As with previous books Steve and I have worked on, his staff and graphics people did an outstanding job. I thank them for their excellent work. Anyone who has written a book knows that it is a labor of love and a consuming force. My best friend, companion, and wife, Nancy, understands that and continues to provide the support and patience that allowed me to accomplish this work.

ONE

At FLETC, trainees learn the safe handling and application of handguns, shotguns, submachine guns, semiautomatic rifles, scoped rifles, and impact weapons. Fundamental training is done on silhouette-shaped targets designed to teach area of aim. After students learn how to shoot, the remaining courses provide realistic training in judgment shooting, trauma management, cardiopulmonary resuscitation, awareness of blood-borne pathogens, water safety and survival, and physical conditioning.

Application

In 2004, the Secret Service introduced a new badge for Special Agents. This was in response to the creation of the Department of Homeland Security and the transfer of the Secret Service into that organization.

The United States Secret Service is mandated by statute and executive order to carry out two significant missions: protection and criminal investigations. The Secret Service is the finest and one of the best-trained executive-protection teams in the world. Its reputation is one of excellence. As one of the nation's oldest general law enforcement agencies, this reputation did not happen overnight but has been achieved because of its highly trained personnel and their dedication, integrity, and love of country. Given that it has one of the most important, sensitive, and serious jobs among its responsibilities—guarding the life of the president of the United States—the Secret Service selects only the most qualified individuals for training.

The most visible position within the Secret Service is Special Agent. The selection and training for this position is now the most demanding in the history of the Secret Service. Applicants must show exceptional intelligence, commitment, physical

In 1875, Chief Whitley asked the Bureau of Engraving and Printing to design a badge for the Secret Service. This new badge is the first appearance of the Service Star, still the emblem of the Secret Service. The badge's five points represent justice, duty, courage, honesty, and loyalty. The first mention in historical records of the badges worn by operatives was during Hiram C. Whitley's tenure as chief in 1869. He issued permission for the operatives to obtain their own badges if they wished to wear them. In 1873, the Secret Service issued standard badges to the operatives, and any previous badges they had could be turned in for a five-dollar credit. Fifteen years later, in 1890, the Bureau of Engraving modified the design for the Service Star, making the badge smaller and easier for the agents to carry in their commission books. When presented, these credentials verified that Secret Service operatives were worthy of trust and confidence.

The modern Secret Service Star

The badge remained unchanged until the Secret Service adopted a new design in early 1971 in response to a move to promote similarity among all Treasury law enforcement badges. The Service's own artists created this badge, and the design is still in use today.

conditioning, and integrity. Today's recruiting policies are designed to reflect the diversity of the American society in which the Secret Service works. Because of the high standards, only about five percent of applicants who receive an initial interview for the Special Agent position will be hired. Most Special Agents will spend twenty years or longer in their careers.

QUALIFICATIONS FOR THE SPECIAL AGENT POSITION

Applicants for the position of Special Agent in the Secret Service must be citizens of the United States. Resident aliens or other noncitizens do not qualify for U.S. Secret Service employment. The applicant must be between the age of twenty-one and thirty-seven at the time of appointment. (In general, there is no age restriction for people in the professional non–law enforcement positions of the Secret Service.) This age range provides law enforcement with the most efficient and effective individuals. The maximum age of thirty-seven at the time of appointment ensures that Special Agents will be able to complete twenty years of service by the age of fifty-seven,

THE MISSON

The U.S. Secret Service, an agency within the Department of Homeland Security, is mandated by statute and executive order to protect the president and vice president, their families, heads of state, and other designated individuals; and to investigate threats against these protectees. The Secret Service also protects the White House, the vice president's residence, foreign missions, and other buildings within Washington, D.C.; and plans and implements security designs for designated national special security events (NSSE). It investigates violations of laws relating to counterfeiting of obligations and securities of the United States; financial crimes that include, but are not limited to, access device fraud, financial institution fraud, identity theft, computer fraud; and computer-based attacks on our nation's financial, banking, and telecommunications infrastructure.

Engraved on the marble wall inside the U.S. Secret Service Headquarters is its motto, "Worthy of Trust and Confidence."

GENERAL ORDERS OF THE SECRET SERVICE

From the beginning, the Secret Service established an atmosphere of discipline, dedication, and integrity. Chief William P. Wood issued six general orders that spelled out an agent's legal and moral obligations:

1. Each man must recognize that his service belongs to the government twenty-four hours a day.

2. All must agree to assignment to locations chosen by the chief and respond to whatever mobility of movement the work might require.

3. All must exercise such careful saving of money spent for travel, subsistence, and payments for information as can be self-evidently justified.

4. Continuing employment in the Secret Service will depend upon demonstrated fitness, ability as investigators, and honesty and fidelity in all transactions.

5. The title of regular employees will be operative, Secret Service. Temporary employees will be assistant operatives or informants.

6. All employment will be as a daily pay rate; accounts submitted monthly. Each operative will be expected to keep on hand enough personal reserve funds to carry on Service business between paydays.

Applicants are required to submit the following initial paperwork when applying for positions: a completed Application for Federal Employment (OF-612); a Declaration for Federal Employment (OF-306); LE 083—Supplemental Qualifications Statement; an SSF 86A—Supplemental Investigative Data; SSF 3289—Statement of Selective Service Status (males only); SSF 3301A—Knowledge, Skills, and Abilities; SSF 3230—Secret Service tax check waiver; and an SSF 3230A—Waiver to permit the Secret Service to obtain one or more credit reports.

which is the mandatory retirement age. Special Agents must serve for at least twenty years to qualify for a retirement pension.

Because of the complex and technical investigations the Secret Service undertakes, its agents must be motivated and well educated. It is preferred the candidate have a bachelor's degree from an accredited college or university, but three years' experience in the criminal investigative or law enforcement fields or the equivalent combination of education and related experience may be acceptable.

Certain law enforcement experience alone will not qualify the applicant for the Special Agent position. Experience as a uniformed law enforcement officer where the principal duties consisted of investigations and arrests involving traffic violations, minor felonies, misdemeanors, and comparable offenses, or in which the major duties involved guarding and protecting property, do not automatically qualify an individual for the position.

The Secret Service may prioritize individual applicants with computer and language skills. Currently (2005), the Secret Service is paying a one-time recruitment bonus of 25 percent of the basic annual pay to newly hired Special Agents who have a foreign language skill and can test at the S-3 level. This level requires that the applicant be able to speak the foreign language with sufficient structural accuracy and vocabulary to participate effectively in most formal and informal conversations on practical, social, and professional topics. The recruitment bonus is paid as a lump sum upon successful completion of all required training and graduation from the Secret Service training academy. To fit certain specific requirements (for example, handwriting or fingerprint experts), the Secret Service may recruit qualified personnel from other government agencies or from state and local law enforcement for technical positions. Male applicants must certify that they have registered with the Selective Service System, or are exempt under the Selective Service law.

Due to physical fitness standards, applicants must be proportionate in weight and height. In an emergency such as an assassination attempt, agents must overcome their natural survival instincts and shield the protectee with their own bodies. It can be strenuous and hazardous duty, and this makes the selection process for applicants extremely demanding. At some point in their careers, Special Agents may be assigned to a protective detail, and the Secret Service wants the best-qualified agents on the protective detail.

The southern view of the White House is as close as anyone can get without a magnetometer clearance. Only specially authorized vehicles are permitted within the 800 feet. The eighteen acres of the White House complex are some of the most protected in the world. *Henry M. Holden*

STEPS IN THE SECRET SERVICE SPECIAL AGENT APPLICATION PROCESS

To become a Special Agent in the U.S. Secret Service, all candidates must first submit a thirty-four-page application, which is downloadable at the U.S. Secret Service website (www.secretservice.gov) or available at local field offices. It may be submitted online via e-mail, sent via facsimile (FAX), mailed in, or hand carried to a local field office.

The application is straightforward, and if the applicant meets the basic requirements of age, education, citizenship, and so forth, he or she will receive a telephone call from the Special Agent in charge (SAIC, pronounced "sack") of the local field office inviting the applicant in for an interview.

"I knew the process was highly competitive," said one agent, "so I began taking Tae Kwon Do and Spanish lessons. I also applied to the San Antonio Police Department and the Texas Highway Patrol, all to give myself an edge over the other applicants."

INITIAL INTERVIEW

The hiring process for Special Agents begins with the initial interview and ends with graduation from the Secret Service training academy. The initial interview lasts about one hour and will determine if the applicant is suitable for the job. It may begin with a supervising Special Agent reviewing the paperwork with the individual. The supervisor will review the job responsibilities with the applicant and make sure the application is complete. The supervising Special Agent will use the application to form the basis of some questions. This interview is not tape-recorded.

Greet the interviewer with a firm handshake, and wait to be told to take a seat. Look directly at the person asking the question, and make frequent eye contact. If there is more than one interviewer, make eye contact with each interviewer over the course of answering the questions. Sit straight, but not rigid. Avoid such nervous mannerisms as frequent crossing of the legs, fidgeting, or excessive folding or unfolding of the arms. Listen carefully to the questions and never interrupt. Speak evenly and distinctly, with a measured meter, level, and tone. Use good grammar and avoid speaking in double negatives, slang, or off-color or inappropriate language. Smile occasionally.

During the initial interview, the supervisor will outline the job responsibilities, including frequent relocation, and possible effects on the applicant's personal life. Throughout their careers, Special Agents may experience frequent travel and reassignments to Secret Service offices located throughout the United States, or in liaison offices in Europe and elsewhere. The applicant is advised to discuss these issues with his or her family and significant others before going any further in the process.

All of the questions during this interview are answerable, and the applicant will be pressed to answer

On the thirty-four-page application for Special Agent, the knowledge, skills, and abilities portion is one of the most critical areas, and requires careful attention to details. It is where the applicant can and should extol his virtues, talents, and skills. Often the applicant fails to make the cut because he did not express himself clearly and cogently in these three areas.
Henry M. Holden

questions he may be reluctant to answer. The agent conducting the interview will keep the interview moving and complete it within the allotted time. The applicant must keep his or her answers concise, since long-winded answers will detract from the applicant's ability to complete the interview satisfactorily.

This interview will not be about the applicant's past but rather how he or she speaks and behaves at the moment. Most of the questions pose hypothetical situations that require a quick assessment of a situation, organization of thoughts, and an articulate answer with a proper course of action.

The primary goal of the interviewer is to learn how the applicant organizes his or her thought process and expresses thoughts. The interviewer is also paying close attention to the applicant's demeanor, regard for the law, and attitude.

KNOWLEDGE, SKILLS, AND ABILITIES

The applicant will be asked to write a series of knowledge, skills, and abilities (KSA) essays demonstrating his or her ability to write logical, sequenced reports. The applicant may be asked to write about his or her experiences dealing with people, accepting responsibility, or making decisions independently or with minimal supervision. Special Agents must be comfortable as team players, and applicants will have to write essays demonstrating their ability to work and deal effectively with both individuals and groups. They must demonstrate an ability to perform Special Agent duties and a willingness to develop a proficiency in the use of firearms and deadly force, if necessary. In addition, they must demonstrate an ability to interpret and follow oral instructions and to present ideas

The Secret Service maintains foreign liaison offices in Paris, France; London, England; Berlin and Frankfurt, Germany; Rome and Milan, Italy; Hong Kong, China; Ottawa, Montreal, Toronto, and Vancouver, Canada; Bogotá, Colombia; Guam; Bucharest, Romania; Mexico City, Mexico; Pretoria, South Africa; San Juan, Puerto Rico; Sofia, Bulgaria; and Bangkok, Thailand.

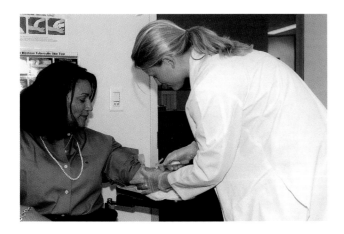

As part of the physical screening, this Special Agent is having blood drawn.

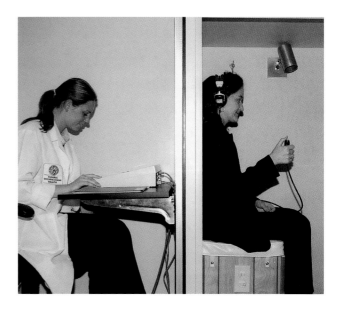

orally. "Applicants have a difficult time writing good KSAs because they do not take the time to detail out their accomplishments," said one agent. "This is the part of the application where they need to brag about their accomplishments, and we can also get a look at their writing abilities."

TIPS FOR A SUCCESSFUL INTERVIEW

Prior research by the applicant about the Special Agent position, and the Secret Service itself, should provide a foundation for the applicant's responses in this interview. "I knew the process was tough," said one agent, "so I did my homework, and called the field office in San Antonio, and spoke to a few agents."

There are things the applicant can do that may lead to a positive outcome. For the initial and subsequent interviews, applicants should appear in business attire.

Politics should be left at home and not constitute part of any response. The applicant's political party affiliation, if any, as well as his or her opinion of the current or recent administrations is inappropriate here. Stereotypical opinions or prejudices toward ethnic or socioeconomic groups should not influence the applicant's responses to questions or scenarios described in the questions. Some of the questions the applicant will face will be related to his feelings and attitudes. For example, "Is breaking the law in the line of duty ever justified? If so, explain with examples." Alternatively, "You are searching an underground parking garage for a fugitive. You pass a locked car and notice a chrome-plated revolver in the back

This Special Agent is undergoing the audio test as part of her physical. Agents must have a full commitment to physical fitness throughout their careers. Special Agents under thirty-three years of age are given physical exams once every three years, while Special Agents forty years of age and over receive physical examinations annually. Additionally, after age forty, special agents are given a stress test biannually. Twice each year, agents must undergo physical fitness tests. They are tested in five areas: push-ups, sit-ups, pull-ups, 1 1/2-mile run, and the sit-and-reach flexibility test. If an agent does not pass these strenuous tests, the service will design a training program to help the agent meet his or her goals.

seat, in plain sight. What steps would you take, in what order, and with what justification?" If the applicant has any knowledge of the search-and-seizure laws, or had a similar experience, he should indicate that his response comes from such knowledge or experience.

This interview will measure many of the skills assessed during later testing, although in a different, formal setting. The applicant will be judged on his or her ability to speak logically and effectively and adapt quickly and easily to a variety of situations.

The applicant will be asked specifically why he wants to join the Secret Service, and if he understands the inherent danger and hardships of the job. There are specific items that will automatically disqualify an applicant from consideration for the Special Agent

A Special Agent is taking notes as he interviews an applicant.

position. They are: conviction of a felony, frequent use of illegal drugs, the sale of illegal drugs, being currently in default on a student or other loan insured by the U.S. government, failure of a urinalysis drug test, any deviant behaviors, failure to register with the Selective Service (males only), financial irresponsibility, or membership in organizations whose intent is to overthrow the U.S. government. At the end of the interview, thank the interviewer and shake hands again.

Every applicant is reevaluated at each stage of this competitive process, and only the most highly qualified proceed to the next step. If the interviewer rates the person above average, arrangements are made for him or her to take the treasury enforcement agent (TEA) exam at the local field office. The TEA is an entrance exam of sorts.

Another agent said, "My attitude was to go out and buy the study guides, and study for the exam to give myself an extra edge to help me pass. I thought, 'Why not go the extra step?' Bettering yourself is the bottom line. Even if I did not pass, I'd be bettering myself." A senior agent said, "This is one of the ways we measure initiative."

TREASURY ENFORCEMENT AGENT EXAM
The TEA covers all applicants for Customs and Border Protection; Alcohol, Tobacco, Firearms, and Explosives; U.S. Secret Service; and Internal Revenue Service enforcement agent positions. There are three parts to the exam: Part A, verbal reasoning; Part B, arithmetic reasoning; and Part C, problems for investigation.

Thorough preparation and common sense are important factors in success on the TEA. Get a good

night's sleep, eat breakfast, go easy on the caffeine, and leave early for the exam to avoid any possible traffic delays. Once the applicant is seated in the exam room, he or she may not leave for any reason until the exam is over more than three hours later. If the applicant leaves, there is no reentry to the examination room.

Part A, verbal reasoning, requires logical reasoning ability and reading proficiency. The applicant must read a paragraph that has all the information necessary to infer the correct answer. The applicant should assume all the information given is true, even if it conflicts with facts known to the applicant. Do not speculate or make assumptions that go beyond the information presented. It is important also to distinguish between essential information and tangential information. The twenty-five short paragraphs are straightforward, but a few may have a twist to them. For example, the applicant must be aware that two negatives make a positive, and that a third negative in the same sentence makes it negative again. There are fifty minutes to read, interpret, and answer the twenty-five questions.

Part B, arithmetic reasoning, does not require the applicant to understand advanced mathematics or memorize formulas. The problems can be solved arithmetically or with simple algebra. It is important to read and reread the problems to be certain exactly what the question is asking. The applicant will be given twenty short verbal descriptions of situations that include some numerical facts. He or she will have to analyze each paragraph, set up the problem, and solve it in a multiple-choice format. The situations may include calculating bank discounts, compound interest, distances, ratios, and proportions. No calculators and only paper and pencils are allowed for this test.

In Part C, problems for investigation, the applicant is presented with a paragraph and several related statements. Clear thinking and concentration are necessary on this important part of the exam. How well the applicant does depends on how well he or she reads. There are sixty minutes allowed to answer thirty questions, but reading speed is not critical to success. Accuracy and careful attention to every detail of each paragraph are important to achieving a high score.

The applicant is encouraged to purchase one of the commercial study guides available to prepare for this test. If the applicant passes this exam with a score of seventy percent or above, his or her paperwork is forwarded to

Recruitment Personnel Security Division (RPSD) in U.S. Secret Service Headquarters. RPSD will notify the field office to call the applicant back for a panel interview with three senior agents.

FACTOR V

Before the panel meets, a "Factor V" (vee) is performed where the applicant signs off on the application, certifying under oath that all statements he or she made on the application are accurate and entirely truthful. The applicant will be asked if there are any incidents in his background, or that of family members, that might lead to blackmail or compromise the applicant's performance as a Secret Service employee. This question is a challenge and requires serious thought to answer accurately. For example, the applicant will need to reflect on every major negative incident that has happened not only in his life, but in the lives of family members, and try to project a future compromising situation.

The applicant will be fingerprinted, photographed, and asked to sign waiver forms for polygraph and drug tests and a background investigation that will begin later in the process. The applicant will also sign waivers allowing the Secret Service to access his tax records and credit reports.

THE PANEL

The one-and-a-half-hour panel interview is designed to solicit additional information from the applicant. This could be stressful for the applicant, because he or she has no advanced notice of the questions, and there are three agents conducting the interview. Throughout their careers, Special Agents will be in stressful situations. The applicant has sworn that statements made on the application are truthful. The panel will review the individual's application for background information. The interviewers may ask general questions and questions of a personal nature. The questions will not be political but will be situational in nature, designed to elicit common-sense answers and to illustrate the applicant's decision-making capability. They may, however, include questions dealing with racial and gender issues to ensure that the applicant does not come to the job with any preconceived prejudices. During this interview, the applicant listens to a specific field scenario and then is asked to write a detailed report of the incident. If two of the three interviewers rate the individual above average or

better, the applicant moves to the next phase, the polygraph.

POLYGRAPH EXAMINATION

The polygraph is one tool in the selection process. It does not detect lies, but measures physiological responses to specific questions. It is used principally to determine an applicant's integrity and truthfulness on issues of national security, illegal drug use, and other information on the application. Like many of the tests the applicant will undergo, it will be stressful and could last about three to four hours.

Before the polygraph is administered, the polygrapher will review the entire process with the applicant. Special Agents and uniformed officers trained at the Department of Defense Polygraph Institute (DODPI) may administer this test. Secret Service polygraphers undergo fourteen to sixteen weeks of training in a course that is standard for all federal polygraphers.

The polygrapher will explain that there are no hidden, secret, or trick questions, and that it should be a two-way process of communication. This test is serious and may have wider implications. The applicant must sign a number of administrative forms as a requirement for the

A polygraph is one tool used in the Special Agent selection process. It is used principally to determine an applicant's integrity and truthfulness on issues of national security, illegal drug use, and certain information on the application. Like all the tests the applicant will undergo, the polygraph is serious, stressful, and may have wide implications.

test. The polygraph may only be employed when the person to be examined has consented in writing to the examination and has been advised of his privilege against self-incrimination. The applicant will be advised that he can stop the test at any time. The polygrapher will also disclose that audio or visual recording devices will not be in use.

Before the actual exam, the examiner will first establish a rapport with the subject. He will ask a number of generic and unrelated questions, and determine if the applicant is physically and mentally sound. Next, he will review all the questions prior to the actual polygraph examination. This is to clear up any questions, or misunderstanding about the questions, and establish a common understanding of what the questions mean.

In order to establish a physiological baseline, the examiner will ask a number of straightforward questions typically answered with a "true" or "false," or "yes" or "no," such as name and date of birth. This baseline is used later to compare the applicant's reaction to essential questions.

Some of the questions relate to personal integrity issues, such as commission of crimes, cheating in school, sexual misconduct, and illegal drug use. The Secret Service does not make its drug policies public, and some drug use in the past may not be automatic grounds for rejection. However, repeated use of hard drugs, such as cocaine, heroin, and steroids, or the sale or facilitation of illegal drugs is grounds for immediate rejection.

In general, federal law enforcement polygraphs follow specific procedures. The applicant will take the actual test, take a brief break, and then undergo the same test again, but with the questions in a different order. The same test questions are administered a third time, and any anomalies between the previous tests answers will be reviewed, and the results put into the selection equation. If the applicant successfully passes the polygraph, he or she will move on to the next phase, the physical examination.

PHYSICAL EXAMINATION

The physical exam, at no cost to the applicant, will consist of a complete physical, including EKG, clinical interview, lab work, screening for past or present chemical or drug dependency, and a complete blood-chemistry workup. In addition, height, weight, body fat, hearing, vision, orthopedic, and neurological screening are necessary to allow the applicant to meet the physical challenges of a wide range of investigative and protective scenarios.

PHYSICAL REQUIREMENTS

The Secret Service is one of the most training-intensive organizations in the world, and agents must maintain a high level of physical fitness. All Special Agent applicants are required to take a preemployment screening exam.

The applicant must be in excellent health and physical condition, and have vision uncorrected no worse than 20/60 (on the Snellen scale) in each eye, correctable to 20/20 in each eye. All applicants must also pass a color vision test. Lasik, ALK, RK, and PRK corrective eye surgeries are acceptable eye surgeries for Special Agent applicants. It is necessary for the Secret Service to retest the applicant who has had Lasik surgery 90 days after the surgery and all other eye surgeries one year after the surgery. If the individual passes the eye and hearing exams, has had a clean drug screening, and has successfully undergone a full medical evaluation, he will move on to the next phase.

HOME INTERVIEW

"No one ever came to my house to interview me for a job," said one agent. The home interview lasts about an hour,

Polygraph results are not admissible in court, but confessions to felonies made because of a polygraph examination are admissible.

The polygraph program is administered by examiners who are highly trained in interview and interrogation techniques. Each examiner is capable of conducting a reliable polygraph examination on issues involving criminal, national security, and employee-screening matters. The polygraph records continuously, visually, permanently, and simultaneously, changes in cardiovascular, respiratory, and electrodermal patterns (blood pressure, heart and breathing rates, and skin responses) and is used to render a diagnostic opinion as to the honesty or dishonesty of an individual.

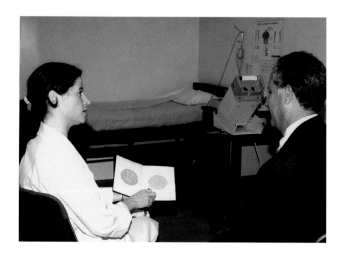

The applicant must have vision uncorrected no worse than 20/60 in each eye, correctable to 20/20 in each eye. All applicants must also pass a color-vision test.

Measuring blood pressure is a necessary test and important throughout an agent's career.

For safety and health issues, each applicant must also pass an audiometer test used to determine whether he meets the minimum hearing requirements. Hearing loss must not exceed: (a) average hearing loss of 25 decibels (ANSI) at 1,000, 2,000 and 3,000 hertz; (b) a single reading of 35 decibels at 1,000, 2,000, and 3,000 hertz; (c) a single reading of 35 decibels at 500 hertz; and (d) a single reading of 45 decibels at 4,000 hertz.

and if the applicant is married, it will include the spouse. The hardships of the job will be discussed in detail—the missed anniversaries, holidays, and birthdays—giving the applicant and his or her family all the information necessary to make an informed decision. "They [the interviewers] answered every question I had," the agent said. "I was so impressed with the process; it helped me decide if this is what I really wanted to do."

BACKGROUND INVESTIGATION

Each applicant will receive a full background investigation that will include in-depth interviews with friends, neighbors, coworkers, teachers, and former employers.

The Secret Service will check every address the applicant has had since birth, go back fifteen years into his employment history, and review his education since high school. If the applicant has lived in many places, or overseas, the background investigation takes longer to complete. If the applicant has relatives living in a foreign country, the Secret Service will call upon the State Department for assistance during the course of the background investigation. The applicant's driver's license record is checked, along with any license inquires.

In conducting the interviews, background investigators place emphasis on specific areas to determine the suitability of the applicant for employment. Some of the areas are:

Character—Does he exercise good judgment and discretion? Is the applicant honest and trustworthy? Is the applicant dependable and stable? Does he have a reasonable temperament?

Associates—With what types of people, groups, and organizations is the applicant involved?

Reputation—What is the applicant's reputation in the community and place of business? Again, the question of honesty arises: Is he honest and does he conduct himself with integrity among his peers and associates?

Financial responsibility—This includes reviewing the applicant's credit history and verifying if the applicant's spending habits are in line with his income.

Other factors, including biases or prejudices, alcohol

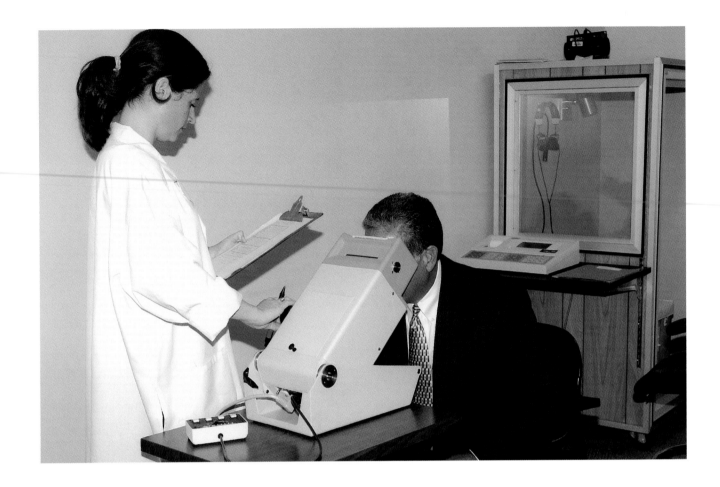

The Secret Service takes excellent eyesight in its agents seriously. There are few occupations where excellent eyesight is so critical to preventing violence or life-and-death situations. These corrective eye surgeries—laser-assisted in situ keratomileusis (Lasik), automated lamellar keratoplasty (ALK), radial keratoplasty (RK), and photorefractive keratoplasty (PRK)—are acceptable procedures for Special Agent applicants. However, the Service will retest an applicant who has had Lasik surgery ninety days after the surgery and all other eye surgeries one year afterward.

abuse, and related behavioral issues, including abuse of prescription drugs, are also part of the background investigation.

When the applicant's input to the process is complete, some individuals sit back and await the results. Others will prepare for the next event in the process: acceptance. "I wanted to be physically prepared beforehand, if I got the call," said one agent. "I worked out three times a week, dividing the one-and-one-half-hour sessions between strength building and endurance. When I got the call to report, I was prepared."

HIRING PANEL

The Secret Service does not make a final decision to hire an individual until it evaluates all the information gathered during the background investigation. The applicant's records are forwarded to a panel of five high-ranking personnel at headquarters. The panel is made up of representatives from the Investigative Division, Human Resources and Training, Protective Operations, Recruiting, and a fifth member from a different division who will act, if necessary, as a tiebreaker.

If the applicant has done his homework and passes the in-depth background investigation on character, honesty, and loyalty to the United States, he will receive top-secret clearance and may be assigned to the field office from which he made his initial application or to another field office, depending on the needs of the Secret Service at the time. At this point, the average age of the new agent appointee is about twenty-seven years. The applicants usually also have a background of significant work experience, discipline, and maturity.

It is a long application process, perhaps twelve to fourteen months. Truthfulness throughout the entire application process is important. Any intentional false statement or willful misrepresentation will result in disqualification. Discovery of misrepresentation after hiring may lead to an inquiry and suitable administrative or disciplinary action, up to and including dismissal.

The candidate has made it over the first hurdle. Now the training in an exciting career that affords a variety of work, challenges, and one that is personally rewarding is about to begin.

Once hired, all employees must maintain their eligibility for a top-secret security clearance, undergo a limited background check every five years, and submit to random drug tests throughout their careers.

The idea of a Secret Service, or a presidential or Praetorian guard, met stiff opposition when it was first suggested. The idea smacked of monarchy, something from which the original settlers were escaping.

LAW ENFORCEMENT ASSISTANCE AWARD

The U.S. Secret Service established the Law Enforcement Assistance Award in 1972. In 1998, the award was renamed the Floyd Boring Award. The purpose of this award is to recognize Explorer Scouts who assist law enforcement agencies with meaningful and exceptional service. Candidates must have performed "an act which assisted in the prevention or solution of a serious crime or an act which assisted in leading to the apprehension of a felony suspect wanted by a law enforcement agency." The award consists of an engraved plaque and a $1,000 scholarship presented by the Retired Agents Society of Secret Service.

BRIEF HISTORY OF THE SECRET SERVICE

1865—The Secret Service Division began on July 5, 1865, in Washington, D.C., when Chief William P. Wood was sworn in by Secretary of the Treasury Hugh McCulloch. Its mission was to suppress counterfeit currency.

1867—Secret Service responsibilities were broadened to include "detecting persons perpetrating frauds against the government."

1875—The first commission book and a new badge were issued to operatives.

1881—President James A. Garfield was shot by Charles J. Guiteau on July 2, 1881.

1894—The Secret Service began informal part-time protection of President Grover Cleveland.

1901—Congress informally requested Secret Service presidential protection following the assassination of President William McKinley.

1902—The Secret Service assumed full-time responsibility for protection of the president. Two operatives were assigned full time to the White House detail.

1906—Congress authorized funds for Secret Service protection of the president.

1908—The Secret Service first protected a president elect. Eight Secret Service agents were transferred to the Justice Department to create what would become the Federal Bureau of Investigation.

1915—President Woodrow Wilson directed the Secretary of the Treasury to have the Secret Service investigate espionage in the United States.

1922—The White House Police Force was created on October 1 at the request of President Warren G. Harding.

1930—The White House Police Force was placed under Secret Service supervision.

1950—Officer Leslie Coffelt, White House Police, was shot and killed by Puerto Rican nationalists while protecting President Harry S. Truman at the Blair House on November 1.

1961—Congress authorized Secret Service protection for former presidents and for the vice president.

1963—President John F. Kennedy was assassinated. Congress authorized Secret Service protection for Jacqueline Kennedy and her children.

1965—Congress extended Secret Service protection to all former presidents and first ladies for life, and to their minor children.

1968—Robert F. Kennedy was assassinated on the presidential campaign trail. He did not have Secret Service protection, but private bodyguards. Congress authorized Secret Service protection for major presidential candidates.

1970—The White House Police Force began protecting embassies around Washington and was renamed the Executive Protective Service. (In 1977, it was renamed the Secret Service Uniformed Division.)

1971—Congress authorized Secret Service protection for visiting heads of a foreign state or government, or other official guests.

1984—Congress enacted legislation making the fraudulent use of credit and debit cards a federal violation. The law also authorized the Secret Service to investigate violations relating to credit and debit card fraud, computer fraud, and fraudulent identification documents.

1994—Congress passed legislation stating that presidents elected to office after January 1, 1997, would receive Secret Service protection for ten years after leaving office. Individuals elected to office prior to January 1, 1997, would continue to receive lifetime protection.

2001—The Patriot Act increased the Secret Service's role in investigating fraud and related activity in connection with computers; authorized the director of the Secret Service to establish nationwide electronic crimes task forces to assist law enforcement, the private sector, and academia in detecting and suppressing computer-based crime; and allowed enforcement action to be taken to protect our financial payment systems, and more.

2002—The Secret Service was transferred to the new Department of Homeland security, effective March 1, 2003.

Two Secret Service agents stationed at the Oyster Bay, New York, summer home of President Teddy Roosevelt carry weapons that are barely concealed in the poorly tailored suits. In 1908, Roosevelt transferred eight Secret Service agents to the Department of Justice. They formed the nucleus of what is now the Federal Bureau of Investigation. The first real test of the Secret Service's protective detail came on February 15, 1933, when Giuseppe Zangara attempted to assassinate President-elect Franklin D. Roosevelt in Miami's Bayfront Park. The president, sitting atop the back seat of a convertible, was unhurt, although several bystanders were wounded, including Special Agent Robert Clark, who was injured in the hand. Chicago Mayor Anton J. Cermak received a mortal chest wound. In one of the shortest periods between crime and execution (thirty-two days), Zangara was executed on March 20, 1933, in Florida's electric chair. Later, the service had a bulletproof railroad car built for Roosevelt. Since the Kennedy assassination, the president has used armored vehicles. At the beginning of World War II, President Roosevelt used an armored car confiscated from gangster boss Al Capone until a specially commissioned vehicle was ready for him. *Library of Congress*

President Grover Cleveland and Vice President Adlai Stevenson ride down Pennsylvania Avenue during Cleveland's inauguration parade in 1893. The only apparent security consisted of a few mounted police and military officers. In 1894, because of kidnapping fears of President Cleveland's daughter, the Secret Service began informal part-time protection. *Library of Congress*

In 1901, President William McKinley was assassinated in Buffalo, New York. He was the third president assassinated in thirty-six years, and the public demanded protection for its presidents. In 1902, the Secret Service assumed full-time responsibility for protection of the president, and two full-time operatives were assigned to the White House detail. The Sundry Civil Expenses Act of 1907 provided funds for presidential protection by the Secret Service. It directed the Secret Service to protect the new president, Theodore Roosevelt. President Roosevelt was the first president to receive official protection. With the assassination of President McKinley, Theodore Roosevelt, not quite 43, became the youngest president in the nation's history. The obvious elevated threat level against a president earned Roosevelt visibly increased security, with three Secret Service operatives accompanying his carriage during his 1905 inauguration parade. Earlier, on September 3, 1902, Operative William Craig was instantly killed in a collision between a streetcar and a carriage in Pittsfield, Massachusetts, while he was riding with President Theodore Roosevelt. President Roosevelt suffered cuts and bruises in the accident. Operative Joseph A. Walker was murdered on November 3, 1907, while working an investigation. He was the first operative killed in the line of duty. *Library of Congress*

President McKinley's assassination created a new attitude about presidential security. The increased security was even more obvious during President William Howard Taft's 1909 inauguration parade. *Library of Congress*

By the time Warren G. Harding became president in 1921, the inauguration parade had gone mechanized. President Woodrow Wilson and President-elect Warren G. Harding are shown in an auto on the way to Harding's inauguration, March 4, 1921. The figure to the right is probably a Secret Service agent. *Library of Congress*

Left: In August 1923, Warren G. Harding died in San Francisco of a heart attack. His vice president, Calvin Coolidge, became president. This photo shows Coolidge and others riding in a car during his inaugural parade. The inaugural crowds had grown by that time, but in this photo, there is no obvious close-in security for the president. *Library of Congress*

Below: President-elect Dwight D. Eisenhower is accompanied by outgoing President Harry S. Truman on the way to Eisenhower's inauguration. Presidential security in 1952 appears to be possibly two agents (in hats) behind the open-top car. Looking back at Truman is Senator Hubert H. Humphrey, who later became President Lyndon Johnson's vice president. On July 16, 1951, Truman said, "The work of protecting me has at last become legal," after Congress authorized permanent Secret Service protection of the president. Until then, Congress had been renewing the authorization to protect the president on an annual basis. *Library of Congress*

Above: Leon F. Czolgosz shot President McKinley with a concealed revolver at the Pan-American Exposition reception, September 6, 1901. During the history of the U.S. presidency, there have been numerous attempts on the life of the president. The first attempted presidential assassination occurred in 1835, when Richard Lawrence unsuccessfully tried to shoot President Andrew Jackson. The government responded by putting a guardhouse and sentry on duty at the White House. Since 1835, there have been thirteen attempts on eleven presidents. Assassins have attacked one out of four presidents and killed one in ten. *Library of Congress*

Above: "Stop that man! He shot the president!" cried a witness when Charles J. Guiteau shot President James A. Garfield on July 2, 1881. The president had been shot, but he was not yet dead. It would take much dirtier hands than Guiteau's to kill President Garfield. When Guiteau, a lawyer with a history of mental illness, shot Garfield in the back, he thought God had told him to shoot the president. But it was not the bullet that killed President Garfield. Over the next few weeks, surgeons tried to locate the bullet in the president's back. Even Alexander Graham Bell tried to help by inventing a metal detector. Unfortunately for the president, the bullet was imbedded so deep in his body that the metal detector could not locate it. Even more unfortunate was that the importance of sterilization in the operating room had not yet been realized. The infection, caused by doctors probing the president's wound with unwashed hands, eventually killed Garfield on September 19, 1881. *Library of Congress*

Above: The man descending the steps behind President and Mrs. Coolidge, drawing on a glove, is James Haley, the Secret Service agent assigned to Mrs. Coolidge. *Library of Congress*

The first photograph of Czolgosz, the assassin of President William McKinley, in jail. Czolgosz, an American anarchist, said that the president was "an enemy of good working people." He was later judged sane, tried, convicted, and executed. *Library of Congress*

While performing a security measure for one of his railroad company clients, Allan Pinkerton (left) ran across a plot to have the newly elected President Abraham Lincoln assassinated before he reached Washington. Pinkerton requested a meeting between himself and Lincoln, and in 1861 the private Pinkerton Detective Agency was given the task of guarding Abraham Lincoln. During the Civil War, there were at least six assassination plots against the president, and Lincoln was the only American president who came under enemy fire while in office. Lincoln was out riding alone to the Old Soldiers' Home a short distance from the White House, when a confederate sniper shot the hat off the president's head. In another incident, during a confederate attack on Fort Stevens in Washington, D.C., on July 12, 1864, Lincoln stood on the parapet of the fort, calmly watching the battle, when he came under fire from a confederate sharpshooter. The sharpshooter, estimated later to be about eight hundred yards away, wounded an army sergeant standing alongside Lincoln. The Battle of Fort Stevens marks the only battle at which a president was present, and under enemy fire, while in office. *Library of Congress*

President George W. Bush shakes hands with American soldiers during his visit to Camp Bondsteel in Kosovo on July 24, 2001. Secret Service agents try to blend in, and while they are noticeable (the men not wearing hats), the crowd has been thoroughly screened before gaining access to the president. *Department of Defense*

The 2006 presidential limousine. The growth of the automobile in the early twentieth century prompted the Secret Service to purchase its first motor vehicle, a 1907 H. White Steamer. However, it was not used by then-President Theodore Roosevelt. The president continued to use a horse-drawn carriage, and the Secret Service used the car as the first follow-up vehicle, behind the horse-drawn carriage. It was not until December 1941 that the first partially armored vehicle joined the presidential fleet. The armor consisted of bulletproof glass, and the vehicle had belonged to Al Capone, who forfeited the vehicle to the government as part of his tax liability. *Cadillac/General Motors*

Stretching and limbering up before exercise is important, especially when one is getting in shape for FLETC.

Inside a purposely unmarked building in Washington, D.C., is the headquarters and research division of the U.S. Secret Service. It is a place where domestic and international operations are monitored and where Secret Service agents and other professional support personnel work to protect America's two most treasured commodities, its currency and its leaders. *Henry M. Holden*

The White House is surrounded with anti-intrusion devices. To the left of the tree in the foreground is a small device that may be a motion detector. *Henry M. Holden*

TWO

Physical fitness is a common goal among all Special Agents. Climbing this wall is only a small part of the training. There is also the not-so-subtle reminder that they must be "worthy of trust and confidence."

Basic Training

The rope line is a potentially dangerous point, and an attack on the principal (AOP) is a scenario agents constantly practice. When the president shakes hands, there is usually a simple barrier separating him from the public. In theory, the magnetometer will pick up any metal objects such as knives or guns, but the Secret Service takes nothing for granted. Agents look for anything out of the ordinary, such as someone wearing a heavy coat on a warm day or someone not smiling. The rope line is highly charged with excitement when the president is within arm's reach, and someone not smiling is someone the Secret Service will watch carefully. The red stains on the trainee's tactical pants are from a paint gun exercise.

The newly selected trainee first reports to his or her local field office and then to the James J. Rowley Training Center (JJRTC) in Beltsville, Maryland, for one week of orientation and evaluation prior to reporting to the Federal Law Enforcement Training Center (FLETC) in Artesia, New Mexico. All applicants for the Special Agent position must attend a nine-week course at FLETC, which serves as an interagency law enforcement training organization for more than seventy-five federal agencies with personnel located throughout the United States and its territories. All federal law enforcement agent trainees, except for those in the FBI and DEA, begin their careers with training at FLETC. It includes instruction in specific law enforcement–related activities, such as nonlethal control techniques (arrest techniques and defensive tactics) and the safe handling, proficient application, and justifiable use of firearms and other weapons.

The instructors at the JJRTC are highly motivated and will devote as much time as necessary to help an individual through the training. The vetting of the applicants

The more exercise an applicant can get before FLETC, the better his chances of success at FLETC.

The FLETC Physical Efficiency Battery (PEB) is a final exam of sorts in the trainee's physical fitness. A passing score is not necessary to receive a FLETC certificate; however, some federal agencies such as the Secret Service require a passing score of eighty-five percent.

PRACTICAL EXERCISE PERFORMANCE REQUIREMENTS (PEPRS)

The student should begin an exercise program long before he or she arrives at FLETC to improve cardiovascular conditioning. Students attending FLETC should be sufficiently physically qualified so not to present an undue risk to the health and safety of themselves and others. All trainees receive medical screening prior to engaging in physical activities and as necessary during the course of training.

during the selection process, and the high caliber of the instructors, results in a very low dropout rate among the trainees.

There are usually twenty-four trainees assigned to a class, and the week will be spent evaluating their physical fitness, swimming ability, and firearms familiarization. They will receive a complete physical exam, including blood pressure and body fat measurements. After medical clearance, they are tested in timed physical activities consisting of a 1 1/2-mile run, pull-ups, and pushups, normalized by gender and age group. Grade results may range from "excellent" to "good," "fair," and "poor."

The firearms familiarization will include untimed and timed firing sequences of about one hundred rounds. The trainee will use a .357-caliber semi-automatic pistol, similar to the one they will be issued when they graduate from training. The standard qualification course for the handgun involves slow, timed, and rapid-fire scores from fifteen yards at a ten-inch circle with five rings scoring from six to ten. The smallest circle (scoring a ten) is two inches in diameter. This familiarization course is designed to teach trigger control. Later, additional training will teach the trainees to become some of the finest expert shooters in the world. The trainees will also learn the nomenclature of the weapon and will be able to break down, clean, and reassemble the weapon.

The last part of the orientation is swimming and water safety. The trainees are evaluated on their comfort level in the water. Nonswimmers will receive instruction

Applicants should be in excellent physical condition before reporting to FLETC, in order to get through the intense physical conditioning that takes place there. They must be sufficiently physically qualified so as not to present an undue risk to the health and safety of themselves and others. All trainees will receive medical screening prior to engaging in physical activities and as necessary during the course of training.

Only the most dedicated and physically fit will survive the fifteen and one-half weeks at the JJRTC.

One sergeant technician on the Emergency Response Team had no law enforcement experience when she joined the Secret Service. "I had never even held a gun," she said. This person had no knowledge of the Secret Service until she heard a graduate school professor talking about their functions in a political science class. "That drew my interest, and since I was in Washington, in school, I applied to the Secret Service for a job.

"They sent me to FLETC, which was an excellent experience. Since I had no law enforcement experience or knowledge of weapons, I needed some work. The first ten days were the toughest; then I began to understand the high expectations they had of us. The instructors were all high caliber, and very knowledgeable, and I wound up getting a good foundation to build on at the Secret Service training academy."

She continued, "I found the instructors at the JJRTC applied more pressure to continually improve on the results I had already achieved. If you are looking for a fantastic job, one with great training, great opportunities, and stability, a job where you can almost do anything with the opportunities, then the Uniformed Division is the place."

FIREARMS TRAINING

At FLETC, fundamental training is done on silhouette-shaped targets designed to teach area of aim. After students learn how to shoot, the remainder of the courses provides realistic training in judgment shooting. Marksmanship is evaluated on a point system. Each student must qualify with a minimum of seventy percent on the practical pistol course. A student who does not achieve a satisfactory level of proficiency in the practical pistol course (210 points out of 300 points, or seventy percent) may take remedial training to correct the deficiency. The total amount of scheduled firearms remedial training offered to students will not exceed eight hours and two retests. Failure to qualify on this course will disqualify the student from the program.

FLETC FINAL EXAMINATIONS

The student is required to achieve a score of at least seventy percent on each of the five written examinations. The student is allocated a total of one hour and forty-five minutes to complete each examination.

FLETC PHYSICAL EFFICIENCY BATTERY

The Physical Efficiency Battery (PEB) is a final exam of sorts in the trainee's physical fitness. It is composed of five events: flexibility (sit and reach test), speed and agility (Illinois agility test), upper body strength (bench press), aerobic capacity (1 1/2-mile run), and body composition (skin fold technique: for males, measured at the chest, abdomen, and thigh; for females, measured at the triceps, suprailium, and thigh). A twenty-five percent or better in each of the first four categories constitutes an acceptable score. The Illinois agility test is conducted indoors. A participant runs through a course that determines the ability to stop, change direction, and run around obstacles. Participants are given two attempts, with the better of the two scored. Each test is age and gender normed. A passing score of seventy percent is necessary to receive a FLETC certificate; however, the Secret Service requires a passing score of eighty percent.

on how to swim, and poor swimmers will be debriefed on what they need to work on. They are told it is up to each individual to improve their swimming techniques, physical conditioning, and other areas they may need to work on, and what physical condition they need to be in when they return from FLETC. Immediately following FLETC, Secret Service trainees return to the JJRTC for fifteen and a half weeks of specialized advanced training.

JAMES J. ROWLEY TRAINING CENTER (JJRTC)

Training in any organization is the backbone of its success. In the Secret Service, historical training has evolved from on-the-job training (OJT) to a highly sophisticated science, providing agents with the most efficient, effective, and up-to-date knowledge available. The James J. Rowley Training Center focuses on specific Secret Service policies and procedures associated with the dual responsibilities of investigations and protection. Instructors will often meet and communicate with other law enforcement agencies and are routinely called upon by such agencies, both foreign and domestic, for their expertise.

"The Secret Service constantly trains for a day we hope will never come," said one training instructor. The JJRTC provides the ideal location, with privacy and security, to conduct such training. Thick forests surround

Upon arrival at the JJRTC for orientation, all nonswimmers will be given instruction on how to swim and poor swimmers will be debriefed on what they need to work on.

the facility, making it almost impossible to see from the roadway, even in the winter. There is no sign announcing the 493-acre compound, located halfway between Baltimore and Washington. Instructors at the JJRTC will teach law enforcement, investigative, and protective skills to new trainees, and refresh the skills of active-duty agents. The point to all the training is to take individuals and mold them into a multitasking team, and to prepare them mentally and physically for one of the toughest jobs in the country. They will learn how to safely perform high-speed driving maneuvers, employ protective methodologies, thwart attempts to harm a protectee, and execute precision marksmanship. They will also learn how to handle themselves in various social situations, from jogging or horseback riding with the president or vice president and other protectees, to formal black-tie affairs of state. (The Secret Service provides, at its expense, all formal wear for male and female agents as needed.)

A training instructor is demonstrating a water rescue using a dummy at JJRTC.

The first formal Special Agent training school was held in 1953. The three-week course covered investigative and protective responsibilities facing the agents of the 1950s. Before that time, training consisted of a tour of the Bureau of Engraving and Printing, a two-week Treasury training program, and informal lectures conducted by various headquarters officials. Agents received the remainder of their training through informal on-the-job training.

CRIMINAL INVESTIGATOR TRAINING PROGRAM

Secret Service agent trainees enroll in the Criminal Investigator Training Program (CITP) at FLETC. The CITP consists of forty training days, excluding weekends and federal holidays. There are 333 course hours in the program, covered in nine weeks of training. The duration of the total program is 357 hours.

Medical conditions that call for a referral to the medical officer include, but are not limited to: epilepsy, diabetes, asthma, emphysema, multiple sclerosis, hypertension, pregnancy, joint injuries/problems, colitis, and heart disease. These conditions are generally indicative of a candidate's inability to satisfy the PEPRs or participate safely in unrestricted physical, weapons, and other training. To participate in training any student with a preexisting condition must bring a copy of any documentation by the attending physician stating the student is cleared for training.

On July 5, 1865, William P. Wood, a former soldier and government official, was sworn in as the first chief of the Secret Service. His job was to restore public confidence in the currency of the United States. Wood recruited ten "operatives," as the early Secret Service agents were called. Most were private detectives or soldiers who had served in the Union Army during the Civil War. During their first year of activity, the operatives arrested more than 200 counterfeiters. By 1875, the Secret Service had restored stability to the country's monetary system.

Colored vests designate trainees who perform different roles. Here they are boarding the Air Force One mockup. The individual in the red vest is the designated protectee.
Henry M. Holden

African Americans make up more than ten percent of the Special Agent corps and about five percent of management. In 2000, of the seven assistant directors, there were two African Americans and one woman. In 2001, Larry Cockell became the first African American promoted to deputy director, the second-highest-ranking agent in the U.S. Secret Service.

The JJRTC is named to honor former Secret Service Director James J. Rowley, who served as the fourteenth director of the Secret Service from 1961 to 1973, and who was instrumental in acquiring and developing the facility. In 2004, JJRTC trained about two hundred Special Agent trainees.

Most of the training is intense, and stressful by design. Trainees and veteran agents will experience simulated attacks repeatedly, so that if the unspeakable happens they will be prepared to act. Their mission is preparation for prevention. Every attempt is made to simulate conditions that may occur in the real world. The plan is to meet any threat with overwhelming force. If there are attempted or successful attacks on political figures in other countries, the Secret Service will attempt to simulate similar conditions and build them into their training scenarios. The new class is encouraged to begin team building, and the first team-building exercise will be to assign a class president to care for administrative duties.

The JJRTC has the tools to make this training realistic and effective. There are moot courtrooms, an indoor swimming tank, retired presidential limousines, the front portion of a Boeing 707 mock-up of Air Force One, a hotel, city streets, and other buildings, all designed to simulate, in a real fashion, possible threat scenarios, and teach agents to respond to attacks and events.

The climate at JJRTC is moderate. Summer temperatures may run into the 90s with high humidity, and during the winter, temperatures may reach the low 20s. Snow is not uncommon from December through February.

Students do not have dorm facilities but are housed in

Special Agent trainees must stay in shape to survive. The instructors will help by running the trainees several times a week. In the right foreground is a training instructor, and at the rear of the formation is another.

nearby hotels, at government expense. Vans transport the class to and from the facility, and trainees will be issued gear for appropriate exercises. The JJRTC is a smoke-free facility.

FIREARMS TRAINING

Firearms training is more extensive for the Secret Service than other law enforcement agencies, and, unlike the training at FLETC, it focuses on the unique issues associated with protective work. The student learns to apply the fundamentals of marksmanship to a new level of speed without sacrificing tactical accuracy. However, the most important component of the firearms training is judgment.

Top: Similar training is also given to trainees for Marine One, the presidential helicopter. *Henry M. Holden*

Right: Physical training and control tactics take up a large block of training. Here instructors demonstrate a defensive tactic in the mat room at JJRTC to President George W. Bush.

Below: Agents must keep themselves in top physical condition in order to pass their reviews.

The standard qualification course for the Sig Sauer .357-caliber handgun involves slow, timed, and rapid-fire scores at a ten-inch circle with five rings, from fifteen yards.

"Simunition," a blank cartridge that has a small paint pellet crimped into the cartridge, can break the skin, so agents and instructors wear protective clothing. *Henry M. Holden*

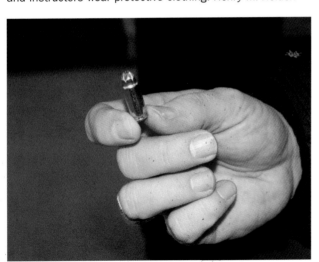

For all training exercises, all students, instructors, and observers wear protective eyewear, and when firearms are involved, hearing protection. Protective clothing is also worn for some firearms exercises where trainees will use "simunition," a blank cartridge with a small paint pellet crimped into the cartridge.

The Secret Service has three basic weapons systems. Special Agents and uniformed officers will qualify on a .357-caliber pistol, an automatic weapon, and a shotgun, and become familiar with other weapons. Part of their training will be a visit to the gun vault, where they will see dozens of weapons ranging from pistols to assault rifles, and one of the latest weapons, a cell phone gun. "As technology increases, so does the number of threat potentials," said one instructor. "We need to show them (trainees) what is out there so they can be ready for a threat in any form. We emphasize 'expect the unexpected.'"

The trainees must be aggressive to succeed as Secret Service agents. They must assert themselves, and throughout their careers they must be able to handle firearms. They will learn to shoot in darkness, and at moving and stationary targets. In an advanced course for the tactical team members, they will learn to shoot from inside a moving vehicle. They will also learn to shoot the "running man," simulations where trainees shoot at a target while it moves across the firing range, and from behind vehicles, using a variety of weapons. Even though it is practice, it is practice with purpose and intensity. That brings reality quickly into the exercise. Trainees will also learn close-protection skills necessary to protect the president and anyone under the protection of the Secret Service.

The standard qualification course for the handgun involves slow, timed, and rapid-fire scores at a ten-inch circle with five rings from fifteen yards, scoring from six to ten. The smallest circle is two inches in diameter. Slow fire is ten rounds in ten minutes; timed fire five rounds in twenty seconds; and rapid fire five rounds in ten seconds. A score of 240 equals seventy percent; for all other firearms courses at JJRTC, eighty percent or higher is passing.

First, however, they will learn to shoot the basic firearms course on an indoor range, in a highly formal and controlled environment, with an expert instructor and range safety officers watching every move the student makes. The student begins with the .357-caliber pistol.

The range officer will command, "In the proper manner draw your pistol—lock the slide to the rear—check the chamber—the magazine well—check, check twice—be sure the weapon is unloaded. In the proper manner, load with twelve rounds. When you put the magazine in your weapon, make sure you give the magazine a pull (to make sure it is locked into position). Shooters, the first round of fire will be two rounds in four seconds." When the shooters have

The Secret Service appointed the first four women as Special Agents in 1971. In 1978, a female Special Agent was assigned to the White House detail on a permanent basis. That same year a female Special Agent was assigned to Vice President Walter Mondale's detail.

In September 2004, thirty-year Secret Service veteran Barbara Riggs became deputy director of the Secret Service. Her appointment marked a significant milestone for the service, as she is the first woman in its 139-year history to serve in that post; currently, she is the highest-ranking woman in law enforcement within the Department of Homeland Security.

The Secret Service combat-threat target qualification score is eighty percent.

Hired usually at the GS-5, GS-7, or GS-9 level, Special Agents' starting salaries are based on the federal government's special rates for law enforcement officers. A candidate with a bachelor's degree from an accredited four-year college or university meets the basic requirement for a GS-5 level. One additional year of specialized experience, superior academic achievement (as defined as a grade point average of 2.9 or higher on a 4.0 scale), or one year of graduate study in a directly related field meets the requirements for a GS-7 or GS-9, depending on qualifications and/or education. Pay scales are adjusted geographically for cost-of-living variations. Local pay adjustments may apply depending on the duty location. Special Agents outside the United States receive ten to twenty-five percent in additional compensation.

Special Agents are also eligible to receive Law Enforcement Availability Pay (LEAP) after the successful completion of training and certification. Under the LEAP program, agents receive an additional twenty-five percent of their base pay due to their availability and frequent requirements to work irregular, unscheduled hours beyond the normal forty-hour work week. Special Agents may rise quickly to GS-12 and GS-13. Newer agents are employed under the Federal Employment Retirement System (FERS) and are eligible for retirement at age fifty, with twenty years of service, or after twenty-five years of service at any age, and must take mandatory retirement at age fifty-seven. Agents must work forty hours per week, and if they are LEAP eligible, must average another ten hours a week. Most agents work between sixty and seventy hours a week, but on a prolonged protective detail that figure may be higher.

The dress code for Special Agents varies according to the agent's activities. For example, an agent on a protective detail will dress in business attire, a dress shirt, tie, and suit for male agents, or suit for female agents. Agents executing search warrants may dress in business attire, or casual or tactical gear and equipment, such as raid jackets, leather gear, and soft body armor, depending on the situation.

The JJRTC training includes, but is not limited to: criminal, constitutional, and civil law; rules of evidence; courtroom procedures and etiquette; how to detect counterfeit currency; credit card fraud; report writing; comprehensive courses in protection; criminal investigation procedures; surveillance techniques; undercover operations; use of scientific devices; emergency medicine; firearms; self-defense measures; arrest techniques and control tactics; extensive physical fitness and conditioning; and protective and defensive driving tactics.

Left: In a simulated attack, ordnance explodes near a vehicle. Reaction time of the Special Agents and the protective team is measured in seconds.

Above: A coordinated attack on the principal begins suddenly with a flash bang detonated near the parade limousine. The secured garage location and the equipment on board the "Beast," as it is called when the commander-in-chief is on board, is a closely guarded secret. The physical defensive mechanisms are also a closely guarded secret, but it probably has multiple layers of bulletproof glass all around, multiple layers of Kevlar, and other blast and ballistic materials on top of, around, and underneath, and it would probably withstand a direct hit from a rifle-propelled grenade. It no doubt contains a self-sealing environment to defend against poison gas; self-contained oxygen system; remote starter; self-sealing fuel tanks; run-flat, bulletproof tires; and wheel inserts that allow the car to be driven and controlled if any of the tires are shot out.

discharged two rounds, the instructor, sitting in a booth that controls the targets, will say, "Come to the ready position. Decock—reholster with one hand against the slide without looking." Agents are taught to draw swiftly and reholster slowly. By the end of this course, the student will have discharged about one thousand rounds.

The largest block of training will be about one hundred hours of control tactics, raid training, hand-to-hand tactics, and reacting to attacks on protectees. The trainees will learn how to control crowds, shield a person they are protecting from gunfire, work a rope line, and escort their protectees. (The rope line is the barrier, often a rope, that separates the president from the crowd when he

A moment before an attack on a protectee, gunmen on the first and second floors can be seen about to spray the motorcade with automatic weapons fire. *Henry M. Holden*

Immediately after the initial shots, a full-scale simulated motorcade ambush takes place. At the same time, another attacker appears in a window near the middle of the motorcade. The Secret Service did not tell this writer when or where that attack was about to happen, but said not to leave the vehicle during the firefight. The "attack" began suddenly and violently, and lasted about twenty seconds. *Henry M. Holden*

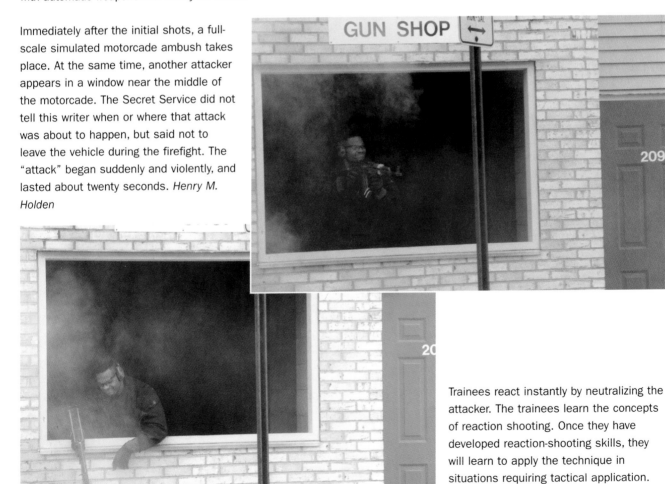

Trainees react instantly by neutralizing the attacker. The trainees learn the concepts of reaction shooting. Once they have developed reaction-shooting skills, they will learn to apply the technique in situations requiring tactical application. *Henry M. Holden*

Trainees move in as a team, covering each other while advancing on the remaining threat. *Henry M. Holden*

Right: Immediately after the simulated exercise, trainees, instructors, and observers gather for debriefing. *Henry M. Holden*

is shaking hands with the public.) In most cases, they will use training weapons as well as other types of firearms for familiarization. These training weapons are modified to fire blank ammunition, or simunition.

Detail agents also participate in a unique simulated crisis training scenario called "AOP," or attack on the principal (anyone under the protection of the Secret Service.) These exercises present Special Agents with a variety of real-world emergencies involving Secret Service protectees, and are designed to provide agents with immediate feedback concerning their responses to the attacks.

FIRST AID TRAINING
All trainees take 40 hours of emergency medical training (EMT) that includes cardiopulmonary resuscitation (CPR), and the proper use of a defibrillator. A defibrillator produces an electrical shock to the heart and is used to stabilize the heart when it is in fibrillation—very rapid, irregular contractions of the muscle fibers of the heart

resulting in a lack of synchronism between heartbeat and pulse. It will not work if the person is not breathing or the heart is stopped. Trainees will also learn to use all the items in the first aid trauma (FAT) kit. The FAT kit includes oxygen bottles, equipment and medicines to treat wounds and burns, splints for fractures, etc. The kit is compartmentalized and clearly labeled.

WATER SAFETY PROGRAM
The water safety program courses include basic water survival, rescue swimming, diving, aircraft safety and evacuation, helicopter emergency egress, and emergency medicine. After the basic course, the students may learn advanced river-rescue techniques. Since agents always accompany the president on helicopter trips, they must be trained to deal with an attack on Marine One, the presidential helicopter. In 1973, an agent on the protective

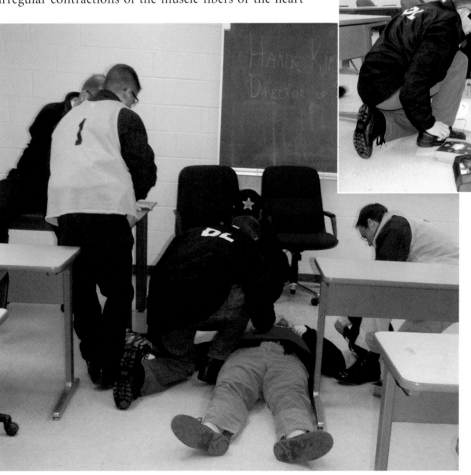

All agent trainees take forty hours of emergency medical training (EMT) that includes cardiopulmonary resuscitation (CPR) and the proper use of a defibrillator. In this simulation, the protectee (in the red vest) had a heart attack. A defibrillator will not work if the person is not breathing or if the heart is stopped, so, for safety, trainees will learn how to apply it to a mannequin instead of a human.
Henry M. Holden

detail died when he was unable to exit the helicopter in which he was traveling when it crashed in the water in the Caribbean. Since then, agents train in simulations of a helicopter going down over water. They practice evacuations where agents are strapped into what is affectionately called a "dunker," a metal container containing a helicopter seat. The dunker is dropped into a pool and rolls over, as typically would happen with a helicopter striking the water. The disoriented trainee must put on a portable breathing device and escape the dunker. The agent, in a real situation, must also assist the president and relocate him to the surface and to safety. In doing so, he may run out of air in his breathing device. He must then call on his antipanic training and replace the device. Eventually the trainee will activate a floatation device strapped to his leg that will send him to the surface. Much of the Secret Service training is designed to suppress and modify normal human responses. The idea is to make everything as real and urgent as possible. The exercises demand total concentration and commitment.

RESCUE SWIMMERS

Some Special Agents who guard a president, vice president, or other protectee around a water environment must also qualify as rescue swimmers. This training goes beyond the day-and-a-half basic water safety segment.

During the basic program, instructors try to drown-proof the trainees for things like aircraft evacuations and situations where they might be going in the water unexpectedly. In addition to basic training, rescue swimmers undergo a two-week program modeled after the coast guard's rescue swimmer program to become certified.

Johns Hopkins (medical) University liaisons are at the Secret Service's Beltsville training location, where agents complete initial medical training and later recertification. Hopkins supports first-responder training for all personnel and advanced training (to the emergency medical technician or paramedic level) for selected agents. On extended overseas trips, they support a team including doctors, nurses, paramedics, and other clinical staff, and offer medical support for government-declared national security special events.

Once a year, the coast guard assists the Secret Service to teach helicopter deployments and rescue devices to selected agents. The training begins with a review of techniques used to rescue a conscious person from the water, with special emphasis on controlling a panicked victim.

Each agent takes turns playing victim and rescuer. The agents practice a very effective method of getting a drowning victim to let go of a rescuer. The rescuer takes a breath, and then goes underneath the surface of the water, taking the panicked victim with him. "The last thing

The indoor swim tank allows year-round water training. Here, an instructor is demonstrating a water rescue.

the person wants is to go back under the water," said the instructor. "We don't fight the victim. We try to get them under control. Then, if they want to tire themselves out, we let them," he said. "We use a cross-hand control technique that allows a victim to thrash from side to side without hindering a rescuer." The swimmers' training will progress to rescuing unconscious and injured victims. The Secret Service is about preventing assassinations, but it is also about medical emergencies. Safety is part of the mission.

BASIC DRIVER TRAINING

The JJRTC's basic driver training program consists of three phases designed to teach vehicle limitations, sharpen skills in recognition of traffic hazards, and improve reflexes and decision-making ability. One phase, defensive driving, consists of negotiating a series of obstacles at slow

In simulations of a helicopter going down over water, trainees practice evacuations. Trainees and personnel on the presidential protective detail (PPD) are strapped into the "dunker," a metal container with a helicopter seat.

Agents will receive specialized water training in case the president is on or near water. Here the coast guard is fishing out an agent who has been in cold-water training. The Secret Service does a lot of specialized training such as scuba diving, and although assassination attempts are unlikely in such an environment, the service takes nothing for granted and still practices AOPs in and near bodies of water. *U.S. Coast Guard*

Left: Safety is a major issue, and even though the Special Agent will not have the benefit of swim goggles in a real emergency, this trainee may be dunked several times before he gets it right. The goggles will help protect his eyes from the chlorine in the water.

The water safety program courses include basic water survival, rescue swimming, diving, aircraft safety and evacuation, helicopter emergency egress, and emergency medicine.

Lower Left: A trainee swims away from the dunker. Much of the Secret Service training is to suppress and modify normal human responses. The idea is to make everything as real and urgent as possible.

speeds. The second phase is skid control, taught on a water-slick skidpan. The third phase of the course is highway response driving.

PROTECTIVE OPERATIONS DRIVING COURSE

One-third of the JJRTC facility is dominated by the protective operations driving course. After the presidential limousines are retired, they are used on the protective operations driving course to teach driving skills necessary for the protective mission. Trainees will be taught specialized driving skills, with emphasis on protective vehicles in motorcade situations. They will learn to negotiate serpentine courses safely through tightly placed road objects, maneuver sharp turns at high speeds, and crash safely through barricades, roadblocks, and other cars. (The nature of this training requires that the vehicles have the automatic braking system disabled.) Instructors can drive the course in just over a minute. All agent trainees will receive three days of driver training, with five days of training for agents on the protective details.

J-TURN

Part of the vehicle-ambush countermeasures training is a scenario where there is a threat in front of a protectee's vehicle. Trainees will learn to get a visual reference in the rearview mirror, and back up a vehicle similar to a Chevy Camaro to about forty miles per hour, then simultaneously, with the left hand, turn the wheel sharply to the right (or left) while shifting to "drive." This maneuver results in spinning the vehicle into a perfect 180-degree J-turn. Without losing any momentum, the driver then guns the engine and speeds off in the opposite direction. This maneuver would only be executed if other protective measures were inappropriate to the situation. These high-speed and evasive maneuvers are first practiced in a highly responsive vehicle, and then the skills are carried over into a less responsive vehicle such as the presidential limousine.

Another escape maneuver is the push out. When the protectee's vehicle is disabled, the vehicle immediately behind that vehicle, which is larger and has a more powerful engine, such as an SUV-type vehicle, pushes the disabled vehicle through turns and obstacles to get the protectee out of harm's way.

TACTICAL VILLAGE AND JUDGMENTAL RANGE

The tactical village and judgmental range look like a Hollywood back lot of Main Street, USA, with streets and

Trainees and agents will learn to safely weave through tightly placed road objects and maneuver sharp turns at high speeds. The course is timed, and while points are not taken off for cones knocked down, two seconds are added to the trainee's score for each cone knocked down.

A car coming out of the J-turn will burn a lot of rubber. The trainees practice on Camaros and similar vehicles, but will also develop the skill on the heavier, much harder to drive, retired limousines. If an attack occurred, the driver could be the most important person in the motorcade. In the crisis of the moment, the driver may have to break through a barricade or execute a J-turn. There may be seconds when the life of the president hangs on the driver's reaction.

several buildings where full-scale protective scenarios are enacted, and where trainees must learn to react to unknown threats. Here, trainees learn to become hypervigilant and highly alert, with the extra edge needed to be successful. The average person's response to a gunshot is to flinch. The Secret Service trains to remove the instinct from the agent and implant a new one: to respond. The response is to cover a protectee and relocate him. "We want to simulate what they might experience in the real world. We don't stand and fight; we get out of there with our protectee," one agent said. The Secret Service has additional personnel on the team who respond to the threat.

The tactical village is designed to provide realistic training in dozens of different situations agents may face. Facades of buildings in the village include a hardware store, restaurant, bar, and bank. Some of the buildings have functional interiors such as offices and businesses, where instructors will simulate crime scenes, practice executing warrants, and interview witnesses.

There are twenty-one pop-up scenarios on the judgmental range where agents on foot and in "motorcades" confront computer-controlled cutout figures that randomly pop up without warning, in windows and doorways. Laser-firing weapons, laser-targeted cutouts, live ammunition, as well as simunition are used, and the exercises are complex and demanding. Controlled by instructors, the cutout figures are movable, bullet-sensitive, and appear at different times, and in different places, carrying a variety of objects. Using a weapon is always a judgment call, and while trainees are taught weapons discipline, they may have a split second to

A small portion of the tactical village and judgmental range, where realistic scenarios are conducted. *Henry M. Holden*

Sudden, violent, and realistic scenarios prepare Special Agents to expect the unexpected. Instructors and hired role players will assault and react to trainees' actions. Simunition and laser-firing weapons may be used to mark bullet wounds on both trainees and instructors.

decide which figures are assassins and which are innocent civilians. They must react by not firing at a nonlethal threat, such as a cutout figure holding what at first glance may look like a gun but is really a wallet or a bottle. The training is designed for the student to use his or her judgment; student must first evaluate, then act. The students are not graded. Instead, they are debriefed after every exercise. The immediate debriefing will include suggestions on how the student can turn a weakness into a strength.

The training exercises are stressful and always unexpected. The trainees know something is going to happen, but they do not know the nature of the threat, nor when or where it will happen. In training exercises, varieties of distraction devices, from firecrackers to larger devices, are used. In a simulation designed to be realistic, one exercise has an "assailant" launching a "flash bang," a pyrotechnic device equivalent to a half stick of dynamite (simulating perhaps a shoulder-fired missile), at a protectee's vehicle from a building window in the tactical village. The ordnance explodes several feet away from the vehicle. Coordination and speed among protective team members are crucial to a successful response to such an attack. These simulations are designed to show agents how to act in such situations. "Throughout the year," said a former SAIC of the JJRTC, "we try to continuously work on making sure that our people are prepared to deal with anything they face. Stepping into the line of fire is a perishable skill, so it requires repetition, and it is

Air Force One mock-up. *Henry M. Holden*

continuous." This skill has to be honed until the agent will react without thinking. In the debriefing that follows every exercise, the trainees will not be scored on the outcome, but instead on what they can do differently next time to affect a better outcome.

One building in the tactical village can be converted into a hotel for simulated attacks in a closed environment. The mock hotel is as real as possible and is used to train agents in the skills they will need in case there is an indoor threat to a protectee. There are different phases of training within the hotel, so instructors can simulate situations an agent may face anywhere in the world.

Trainees will learn to work the rope line as a protectee greets the public. In this setting, undercover agents are

A February snowstorm left a blanket of snow on the cover course. There, two trainees, using the available cover, try to make it from one end of the course to the other without getting shot with paint balls fired by an instructor.
Henry M. Holden

Simulated attacks that produce this kind of pyrotechnics and debris are about as close to the real thing as anyone can get.

moving within the crowd along with the protectee. Other agents and trainees are watchful for a threat from the crowd. "There is no particular profile for a presidential assailant," said one agent. "Except for the attacks on Presidents Nixon and Ford, where the assailants were female, all the assailants have been white, between the ages of twenty and forty, and all small in stature. We teach them to 'expect the unexpected, every time,'" he said.

COVER COURSE

In the cover course, two agents will try to make it from one end of the course to the other without being "shot" (with paint balls fired by an instructor). The course is about thirty feet long, and there is not much cover: a fire hydrant, a newspaper vending machine, a small wall, a tree, and a fifty-five-gallon drum. They will have to move fast, and do it as a team, covering each other as they move forward. "They have to be the best at what they do," said one instructor. "And we feel they are. That is the edge we are constantly trying to give them."

BELTSVILLE FIELD OFFICE

The Beltsville field office (BFO), located on the training center grounds, is a mock-up of a typical Secret Service field office. The trainees will spend the last two weeks of their training applying what they have learned to new real-world simulations.

The trainees split into two-person teams and will work with minimum supervision. They will now have to rely on their training to solve some simulations modeled after actual events. Hired role-players are used for some simulations such as counterfeiting, as well as in scenarios for developing interviewing techniques, but only instructors and other Special Agents are used for raids and other physical training.

To be an effective interviewer takes practice and skill. The BFO contains interview rooms with video feeds to other rooms, where trainees observe proper interview techniques. Instructors will role-play the part of detainee, and trainees practice the art of being an effective interviewer. Videotape equipment is used extensively in practical exercises on interviewing a witness so that students can play back the tapes made of their interviews prior to the instructor's critique. Debriefs will occur after each simulation, and the trainees will find out what they did right and what opportunities they missed. The BFO

The trainees in the Chevy Suburban ahead are part of a simulated motorcade. They have no idea when, where, or even if an AOP will take place, but in this motorcade, one did five minutes later. *Henry M. Holden*

contains virtually everything a field office would have, from microscopes and other technology used to detect counterfeit currency, right down to a first aid trauma kit.

ADVANCE TEAM TRAINING

While it may be several years before a trainee is part of a protective advance team, he or she will have an opportunity to plan a simulated advance involving a protected visit at an unspecified location outside the training center. The instructors will "chalk talk" the event, and use video and other visual aids to plan the event. They will then walk the trainees through the location, pointing out what arrangements must be made, such as deploying countersnipers and bomb-detection squads. That evening the trainees are given the actual off-site location in a nearby town where they will be tested the following day. This off-site training may last two weeks. "This is where all the training segments come together," said one agent. "The trainee now sees how the entire team works together."

Teamwork is critical to the agent's success in the mission. Trainees will play different roles, so if the president or other protectee is ever harmed, the agent can respond instantly and be prepared do whatever is necessary to remove the protectee from harm's way—subdue the assailant, call ahead to the hospital, drive to a safe and secure place, or control the public at the scene.

Special Agents do not work their way up the ladder of advancement by staying in one field office. They transfer between field offices and at some point may get an assignment to the Washington, D.C., area to develop further management skills. From time to time, they will work on joint task forces with Alcohol, Tobacco, Firearms, and Explosives; U.S. Customs and Border Protection; local police; and IRS offices. For instance, an agent may start in the Chicago field office, move to the protective detail, and then to the Miami and Houston field offices, before entering the management ranks, which is generally at the GS-14 level as assistant to the Special Agent in charge (ATSAIC, pronounced "at-sack"). A field office like Chicago may have a hundred or more Special Agents, plus ten in the Milwaukee resident office (RO), ten more at the RO in Springfield, Illinois, and three in the resident agency (RA) in Madison, Wisconsin.

EQUIPMENT

Secret Service agents are issued a pager, cellular phone, a credit card to cover gas expenses, laptop computer, a pistol as a duty weapon, and soft body armor. A car equipped with law enforcement communications equipment and shoulder weapons (shotgun or automatic weapons) is available, based on the agent's assignment.

The JJRTC will test the trainees' reaction time, and they will be tried and tested again and again. They will have to rely on all of their reflexes and their physical, mental, and moral strength. When they report for field office duty, they will take with them a confidence and a self-assurance that can only be earned, never bestowed. However, advance team training is only the first step. Agents will return to JJRTC for refresher courses several times during their careers.

GRADUATION

After successfully completing the JJRTC course, trainees are sworn in as probationary Special Agents for one year. Upon completion of that year, they are put on two-year provisional status. At the end of the satisfactory completion of that period, they are granted career status.

The new agent's training does not end at graduation. Agents will continue to receive firearms requalification. In the Washington, D.C., area, agents must qualify every month with their handgun and quarterly on the shotgun and automatic weapon. Agents in other field locations will requalify on all weapons quarterly. They will also take emergency medicine courses, refreshers on undercover operations techniques and advanced-access-device fraud (ATMs, etc.), training in new laws that affect law enforcement, and more. Such continuous training has led to a ninety-nine percent trial conviction rate, which is a testimony to the agents' familiarity with the law and criminal procedures.

Fitness is important in the Secret Service, and it is up to the individual to maintain fitness skills at a high level throughout his or her career. Every field office has either a gym or a contract arrangement with a local gym where agents can exercise. Agents are allowed three hours a week of on-duty time for exercising if operation requirements permit. Good physical conditioning is part of the agent's overall yearly evaluation.

Above: This Special Agent is requalifying on the Remington 870 shotgun.

SPECIAL AGENT OATH

(I swear) I will support and defend the Constitution of the United States against all enemies, foreign and domestic; that I will bear true faith and allegiance to the same; that I take this obligation freely, without any mental reservation or purpose of evasion; and that I will well and faithfully discharge the duties of the office on which I am about to enter. So help me God.

Agents must requalify on their issued pistol at least four times a year. Originally, Special Agent handgun qualification took place on a small range in the basement of the U.S. Post Office on Pennsylvania Avenue in Washington, D.C. Today, the quarterly qualification is an eight-hour session in which the agent runs through the various judgmental courses. Agents have only a fraction of a second to decide who the perpetrator is, and who the innocent civilian is. This is why the Secret Service makes all its agents the best shooters in the world. Some day they may find themselves looking into a crowd of innocent civilians and they have to hit the right target the first time.

Practice AOP scenarios are constant at the Beltsville training facility for agents assigned to a protective detail.

Above: Another section of the tactical village and judgmental range is a series of empty buildings used as a backdrop for simulated attacks on unsuspecting trainees.

Below: The Secret Service continually trains its personnel under the most realistic conditions possible.

One team is designated to relocate the protectee and others are assigned to meet and neutralize the threat.

Special Agents must know how to restrain a suspect quickly and safely.

The suspect is being covered by a trainee with an automatic weapon and told to drop his AK-47 assault rifle. The Secret Service uses weapons they know terrorists have and, given a chance, will use.

New agents will learn there is a Secret Service culture of speaking, acting, writing, and dressing. This will also include developing a life-long work ethic of being detail-oriented, efficient, and worthy of trust and confidence.

Learning how to step off a moving limousine is a skill that can be learned quickly. Scanning a crowd and spotting a threat is a skill that requires time, practice, and field experience. This is why classroom study is supplemented with on-the-job training. New Special Agents will be assigned to one of more than 132 Secret Service field offices, where the SAIC will assign a mentor senior agent to the new agent. All agents receive the same type of training during this first year. They will work with experienced Special Agents on investigative work (counterfeiting, ATM fraud, forgery, etc.) and protective work, depending on the needs of the Secret Service at the time. Field office investigative experience is considered essential to the developmental process that will eventually equip a Special Agent with the tools to work on a protective detail. It has long been the belief within the Secret Service that the powers of observation, assertiveness, and the ability to read people are gained in field assignments and are the tools that make for an effective protective agent.

THREE

Uniformed officers and honor guard stand at attention prior to the funeral of former President Ronald Reagan.

Uniformed Division

The uniformed officer's badge depicts the Uniformed Division's major responsibility: protection of the White House.

The White House is a symbol of the United States and the American presidency. Every entrance to the White House is monitored twenty-four hours a day by various sensors. However, the most serious and effective security shield is not the technology, but the men and women of the United States Secret Service Uniformed Division (UD). They work alongside Special Agents and are responsible for the safety of the White House residents and the integrity of its security. The Secret Service Uniformed Division, along with the Metropolitan Police Department and the U.S. Park Police, patrol the streets and parks near and around the White House.

The Uniformed Division, initially a force composed of a few members of the military and the Washington, D.C., Metropolitan Police Department, began formalized protection of the White House grounds in 1860. In 1922, the group became the White House Police Force, with its responsibility to protect the White House and the surrounding grounds. It was not until 1930, after an unknown intruder managed to walk into the White House dining room, that President Herbert Hoover recognized the need for the White House Police and the Secret Service to join forces.

In 1970, the Secret Service's responsibilities increased significantly when Congress authorized the White House Police to protect foreign diplomatic missions in the Washington, D.C., area, and renamed the force the Executive Protective Division. The name changed again in 1977, when it became the U.S. Secret Service Uniformed Division. Today, the Uniformed Division is composed of four branches: the White House Branch, Foreign Missions Branch, the Naval Observatory Branch, which protects the residence of the vice president, and the Special Programs Branch.

A motorcade is exiting the east gate. Everything comes to a stop when a motorcade exits the White House. All traffic is stopped and blocked, and pedestrians are also asked to remain where they are until the motorcade clears the area. *Henry M. Holden*

The Secret Service Uniformed Division is sometimes compared to a police force. However, unlike a police force, Uniformed Division officers' main mission is protection. They accomplish this mission through a network of fixed posts, vehicular and foot patrols, and the Special Programs Branch, which plans for special events, interaction with tourists, state dinners, bill signings, and other units such as countersniper (CS) teams, emergency response teams (ERT), and canine units.

The Uniformed Division is constantly on the watch for any disturbances or suspicious or criminal activity. It conducts regular patrols to monitor the grounds, buildings, and security equipment. Officers are assigned to fixed security posts at entrance and exit points to ensure that visitors are authorized to be on the premises. They operate magnetometers at the White House and other sites to prevent persons from taking unauthorized items into

When the Uniformed Division's bicycle patrol is not constantly in motion around the White House gates, the officers are answering questions from tourists. While they have a serious job of helping to maintain the security of the White House, they are also courteous and helpful to the tourists. *Henry M. Holden*

At least one motorcycle officer will ride the point in a motorcade. A moment later, the motorcade of about ten vehicles followed this officer. *Henry M. Holden*

There are only two entrances open to the White House. Here, the east entrance is heavily barricaded with Jersey barriers, allowing only a single vehicle to pass at a time. Only authorized vehicles are allowed past this point, and they will be stopped at several checkpoints and inspected for explosives and other unauthorized materials and weapons.
Henry M. Holden

The first checkpoint at the southwest gate of the White House is a formidable obstacle. The steel barrier with the stop sign is positioned at an angle to repel any vehicle attempting to break through the gate. It is lowered if the vehicle has authorization. A series of serpentined Jersey barriers also forces a vehicle's driver to slow down to a crawl to enter the area. *Henry M. Holden*

secure areas. They have the authority to question, search, and arrest trespassers or others involved in illegal or disruptive activities.

QUALIFICATIONS

Applicants for the Uniformed Division must submit to the same process as Special Agent applicants and meet most of the same qualifications as the Secret Service agent position, except the applicant must have a high school diploma or equivalent. Applicants for the Uniformed Division must be U.S. citizens, with a valid driver's license, and qualify for top-secret security clearance. Applicants must be between twenty-three and thirty-seven years of age when appointed to the Uniformed Division officer position. Prior to consideration, applicants must pass a written exam. Qualified applicants will then receive a personal interview and must complete a polygraph examination, background investigation, and credit check as a condition of employment.

"I joined the service at the age of 29," one officer said. "I think by that age I had the maturity to understand the awesome responsibility I was given." As far as recruiting others for the service, he says, "The service is very selective. I know some young people who have a lifestyle that would not get them far in the employment process. If I think the person can pass the background and drug test I might recommend they take the test."

The second checkpoint on the southwest gate of the White House has fewer physical barriers than the first checkpoint but it is still a stop-and-check-IDs point. Only specifically authorized vehicles are permitted to reach this point. *Henry M. Holden*

Applicants must submit a thirty-four-page completed primary application similar to that for the Special Agent position to the local field office, or via mail, e-mail, or facsimile (FAX) to headquarters. If the applicant meets the basic competitive requirements of age, education, and citizenship, he or she will be called to the local field office for an initial interview. There are specific issues on the application that will automatically disqualify an applicant from consideration for the uniformed officer position. They are as follows: conviction of a felony; frequent use of illegal drugs; the sale of illegal drugs; currently in default on any federal debt, such as income tax or a student loan insured by the U.S. government; or failure to register with the Selective Service (males only). Financial irresponsibility or membership in organizations whose intent is to overthrow the U.S. government will also disqualify an applicant. If the applicant has engaged in any of these behaviors and does not disclose them, the polygraph, taken later in the process, will reveal them, and the applicant will be rejected. Any deception on the application discovered after the applicant is hired may result in dismissal of the employee and possible criminal charges.

Looking at the southwest gate from the inside, one can see that the steel barrier up and to the left is part of the Jersey barrier that forces vehicles to slow down. *Henry M. Holden*

Tourists line up under the watchful eye of a Uniformed Division Bicycle Patrol Unit officer at the only White House entrance open to the public, located off the east wing.

A uniformed officer interviews an applicant. The Secret Service is very selective in whom it employs.

KNOWLEDGE, SKILLS, AND ABILITY

Part of the initial written application process is the completion of the knowledge, skills, and ability (KSA) portion of the application. Similar to the Special Agent application, it will ask the applicant to describe and elaborate on eight criteria important to successful performance as a uniformed officer. The extent to which the applicant possesses these factors will be evaluated based on the applicant's responses. The applicant's responses should not be bashful, but should instead take pride in his or her knowledge, skills, and unique abilities. It is an opportunity for the applicant to provide valuable firsthand input needed to assess his or her qualifications. Applicants for the Uniformed Division officer position should not relate routine protective duties they may have performed in the past in responding in this part of the application. These job factors are considered automatically.

The application will include a waiver to permit the Internal Revenue Service to release information to the Secret Service about the applicant that would

The Uniformed Division badge has a history of changes. The first badge appeared in 1922, the year the White House Police Force was formed. Through the years, the badge has had seven renditions, each changing with the era, the name, and the responsibilities of the force. The current badge came into existence in 1977.

otherwise be confidential. There is also a release for the Secret Service to obtain one or more consumer credit reports about the applicant.

WRITTEN TEST AND INTERVIEW

Because this phase is critical to success in the process, it is important that applicants carefully read the information on the Secret Service website concerning all aspects of the Uniformed Division officer position. The process includes an informational briefing and test administration; if applicants successfully complete the test, a personal interview may be given. Applicants should wear appropriate business attire and must bring a valid driver's license to the test. If the license does not have a photo, the applicant must provide an additional form of photo identification. During the process, the applicant will be fingerprinted.

The next step is a personal interview, which will be used as an assessment tool in the process prior to hiring the individual. The questions are tough, pointed, personal, and uncompromising. Vague responses will usually result in tougher questions or repeating questions until the applicant answers satisfactorily. The best way to overcome the fear of the interview is prior preparation. Try to anticipate some of the questions. For example, "Why do you want to be a uniformed officer in the Secret Service?" Or, "Do you understand the dangers of the job?"

An impressive performance in an interview will move the applicant to the next phase. In addition to being able to describe on the KSA portion of the test why he is the right person for the job, the applicant must be able to verbalize this. An impressive work background is one factor, but the impression the candidate leaves with the interviewer will be crucial in determining his or her advancement to the next step in the process. Applicants should be prepared for an interview lasting approximately four hours.

If the applicant passes the personal interview, the Secret Service will arrange for the applicant to take the Police Officer Selection Test (POST). Prior to taking the examination, it is highly recommended that the applicant obtain one of several comprehensive police officer test preparation guides available from bookstores or online.

POLICE OFFICER SELECTION TEST (POST)

The POST is an entry-level basic skills test that helps law enforcement agencies select the most qualified applicants. It ensures that candidates possess the basic cognitive skills

---

PRELIMINARY APPLICATION PACKAGE FOR UNIFORMED DIVISION POSITIONS INCLUDES THE FOLLOWING:

· OF 306—Declaration for Federal Employment
· OF 612—Optional Application for Federal Employment or Resume
· SSF 86A—Supplemental Investigative Data
· SSF 3301A—Knowledge, Skills, and Abilities

The Magnetometer Unit personnel, part of the Uniformed Division, detect and prevent potentially dangerous items and unauthorized weapons or items from entering a Secret Service-secured area. This unit also supports the Secret Service's protective details.

---

necessary to perform in a law enforcement position successfully. This is a job-related test, designed specifically for law enforcement use, that measures the basic skills of arithmetic, reading comprehension, grammar, and incident report writing.

While it is helpful to have a police officer background, it is not necessary for the POST. There is a federal mandate that one is not required to know police procedures when taking part in a federal law enforcement exam process. Many police procedural questions on the POST are common sense, and others are usually included in the interview in some form. The reason for this is that they measure two very important traits needed for police work: judgment and common sense.

If the applicant passes the POST with a seventy percent or higher score, he or she is scheduled for the panel interview. The same general guidelines for the Special Agent applicant apply here. Later, the applicant will receive the same polygraph, background investigation, credit check, and medical exam as the Special Agent applicant. Because of the high standards and low attrition rate, only about five percent of the applicants will be hired to the Uniformed Division.

TIPS

Assuming the applicant meets the educational requirements, one should still prepare for the interview and test by doing some research and homework. Call a local Secret Service field office. Find out what they can share about the position. Visit a location (if possible) where uniformed officers work, and learn about them. Ask what a uniformed officer does and specifically what skills, knowledge, and abilities are required. The KSA form will have specific areas the applicant can research and be prepared to answer. One question that may be asked at the interview is, "What do you know about the Uniformed Division of the Secret Service?" So it is important to do as much research as possible.

BACKGROUND INVESTIGATION

Each applicant to the Uniformed Division will undergo a full background investigation. The Secret Service will check every address the applicant has had since birth, go back fifteen years into his employment history, and verify his education since high school. The applicant's driver's license record is checked, along with any license inquiries. In-depth interviews with friends, neighbors, coworkers, teachers, and former employers are also part of the process. If the applicant has lived in many places, or overseas, the background investigation takes longer to complete. In conducting the interviews, background investigators place emphasis on specific areas in determining the suitability of the applicant for Secret Service employment. Some of the areas are character, associates, reputation, and financial responsibility, as discussed in Chapter One.

MEDICAL EXAMINATION

Applicants must pass a comprehensive medical examination, which is provided at no cost to the applicant. The applicant must be in excellent health and physical condition, have vision no worse than 20/60 (by the Snellen standard) uncorrected, and 20/20 in each eye when corrected. Corrective eye surgeries that are acceptable procedures for uniformed officer applicants are laser-assisted in situ keratomileusis (Lasik), automated lamellar keratoplasty (ALK), radial keratotomy (RK), and photorefractive keratectomy (PRK). (Note: Lasik, ALK, RK and PRK corrective eye surgeries have been deemed as acceptable for applicants provided they pass specific visual tests one year after surgery. Applicants who have undergone Lasik surgery may have visual tests three months after the surgery.) All applicants must also pass a color vision test, and their weight must be in proportion to their height.

Twice each year, uniformed officers must undergo physical fitness tests. They are tested in five areas: push-

Uniformed officers serve as firearms instructors and classroom instructors in the JJRTC. They are involved in all training programs and the Secret Service's Post Office Range in Washington. The programs include protective operations driving, arrest techniques, defensive tactics, emergency medical care, and more.

The Uniformed Division began with a few members of the U.S. military and the Washington, D.C., Metropolitan Police Department. Formal protection of the White House and its grounds began in 1860. During the Civil War, the "Bucktail Brigade," soldiers from the 150th Pennsylvania Volunteer regiment, and four Washington, D.C., police officers were assigned to guard the mansion. In 1922, at President Harding's urging, Congress passed legislation that established a separate organization of thirty-three men called the White House Police Force. The statute created the force "for the protection of the Executive Mansion and grounds." The members of the force would have privileges, powers, and duties "similar to those of the members of the Metropolitan Police of the District of Columbia." In 1930, the true precursor of the Secret Service Uniformed Division began after an unknown intruder managed to walk into the White House dining room. President Hoover wanted the Secret Service to exclusively control every aspect of presidential protection, so Congress placed the supervision of the White House Police under the Chief of the Secret Service. The Executive Protective Service was officially renamed the Secret Service Uniformed Division on November 15, 1977.

ups, sit-ups, pull-ups, 1 1/2-mile run, and the sit-and-reach flexibility test. If an officer does not pass these strenuous tests, the service will design a training program to help the officer meet his or her goals.

UNIFORMED OFFICER TRAINING

Initially, the uniformed officer trainee will report to the Washington, D.C., field office of the Secret Service for two weeks of orientation before reporting to FLETC. Following successful completion of the intensive eight-week basic police training course at FLETC, the uniformed officer trainee will move on to specialized instruction at the Secret Service training center in Beltsville, Maryland. Training includes coursework in police procedures,

Motorcade Support Unit (MSU) provides skilled motorcycle tactical support during motorcade movements for the president, vice president, and other protectees when they travel in Washington, D.C. This includes escort, traffic control, and safe, unhindered transportation for protectees.

SOME QUESTIONS ON THE POST TEST MAY BE (ANSWERS IN BOLD):

1- You arrest a burglary suspect and handcuff him with his hands behind his back. What do you do next?
  a.) Check the back seat of the squad car where the suspect will be seated to see if there are any weapons.
  b.) Advise the prisoner of his Miranda rights.
  c.) Search the prisoner.
  d.) Place the suspect in the back seat and seatbelt him.

2- What is one factor in deciding whether nondeadly physical force is reasonable?
  a.) religion
  b.) social status
  c.) age
  d.) race

3- What is the most dangerous part of a domestic disturbance call?
  a.) making an arrest
  b.) interviewing the individuals involved in the disturbance
  c.) approaching the scene
  d.) transporting a prisoner

Vehicle Inspection Team officers work alongside canine explosives detection teams in conducting physical searches of all vehicles entering the White House complex.

The Special Operations Section (SOS) is a specialized unit of the Presidential Protective Division's White House Branch. Uniformed Division officers assigned to this section are trained to handle special duties and functions at the White House Complex. These duties include conducting the daily Congressional and public tours of the White House, and handling events such as state dinners and official arrival ceremonies for foreign heads of state.

A graduating class of uniformed officers. They are reminded by the banner overhead that their job, like that of the Special Agent, is worthy of trust and confidence, and they must maintain the same high standards.

psychology, police-community relations, criminal law, first aid, laws of arrest, search and seizure, and physical defense techniques. Classroom study is supplemented by on-the-job training and, later, advanced in-service training programs. Firearms accuracy and physical fitness training are stressed in the training and throughout the officer's career.

Uniformed officers serve as one line of defense against White House intruders and at other designated locations. They will rotate tours of duty in the various branches to obtain comprehensive knowledge of all aspects of the Uniformed Division's responsibilities. Assignments are competitive in specialized units such as Countersniper, Canine Explosive Detection Team, Emergency Response Team, Crime Scene Search Technicians, Special Operations Section, and vehicular and motorcycle patrols.

SECRET SERVICE CANINE PROGRAM

In 1975, the Secret Service began its canine program when it realized the canine and its handler were the most effective means of detecting explosives. The Secret Service uses Belgian Malinois (pronounced MAL-in-wah) canines bred originally in Holland but now bred in the United States. This breed is about the size of a German shepherd, has short hair, and works well in hot weather. The Malinois is fast, has a strong bite, and is very sociable. During the basic training of the "green dogs," they are taught obedience using hand and verbal signals, scent scouting, tracking (ground scent), article search, and the detection of both high- and low-vapor explosive odors. The ideal dog is one that is hyperactive, with the energy and stamina needed for exhaustive searches. Although they have strength and endurance on the job, most dogs quiet down at home, away from the work environment.

One canine technician was recruited directly from the United States Marine Corps, where he had served embassy duty and was exposed to Secret Service agents. "I found the [Secret] Service a unique way to continue to serve my country," he said. "It was a continuation of my Marine

Corps oath, to serve and protect, and I could see history in the making."

Canine training takes about seventeen weeks, and during the first month, the dog remains at the kennel, giving it and its technician a chance to bond. After that period, the animal goes home with the technician at the end of his shift and remains with the technician twenty-four hours a day. The canine becomes a member of the family.

Both animal and technician must successfully complete the course together. After graduating from initial training, each canine retrains about eight hours every week for the rest of its career.

Canines will work all venues that the president, vice president, or other Secret Service protectees will visit. The 2004 Republican National Convention at Madison Square Garden and the Democratic National Convention in Boston, with thousands of possible spots to hide an explosive device, are just two of the many areas where the canines recently performed exactly to their training. During such trips, the Secret Service may also use military dogs. Explosive ordnance disposal (EOD) personnel from the navy and army are attached to the Secret Service as needed.

Even Secret Service vehicles are checked at a protected venue. "We don't take anything for granted," said one technician. "If a Secret Service vehicle is entering a secure area, we will have a dog check it out before it enters. If the vehicle was not in a secure location we can't guarantee it is threat-free."

The average retirement age for a canine varies depending on its physical condition, but for most dogs, it is about ten years of age. When a canine is ready to retire, it generally retires to the technician's home.

COUNTERSNIPER TEAM

The Secret Service countersnipers are highly trained rifle sharpshooters who assist in providing a secure environment for the president and other protectees. They are trained with specially designed sniper rifles and other

continued on page 79

All Secret Service agents and uniformed officers will undergo some type of raid training under the most realistic conditions possible.

ERT members demonstrate automatic weapons to President George W. Bush.

PROFESSIONAL POSITIONS WITHIN THE SECRET SERVICE

- Accountant
- Architect
- Attorney
- Budget analyst
- Chemist
- Civil engineer
- Contract specialist
- Electronics engineer
- Materials engineer
- Nurse consultant
- Operations research analyst
- Procurement analyst
- Research psychologist
- Forensic expert
- Polygrapher
- Intelligence specialist

SECRET SERVICE TECHNICAL POSITIONS

- Computer specialist
- Photographer

OPERATIONS SUPPORT TECHNICIANS

- Protective support technician
- Fingerprint specialist
- Access control officer
- Document analyst
- Telecommunications specialist
- Physical security specialist
- Special officer

These positions are associated with the direct support of professional or administrative personnel. The work is generally nonroutine in nature and involves extensive practical knowledge either gained through on-the-job experience or specific training at a level equal to or less than that represented by a college education.

ELIGIBILITY

- An applicant tentatively selected for a position must submit to urinalysis screening for illegal drug use prior to appointment.
- Actual appointment will be contingent upon the receipt of a negative drug test result.
- All Secret Service positions require a top-secret security clearance. Some positions require the applicant to take a polygraph examination.
- An applicant must be a citizen of the United States.

The canine unit responds to bomb threats and suspicious packages. The unit performs security sweeps and material examinations to provide a safe and secure environment for persons and locations that the Secret Service protects. The unit also supports the protective details. The canine technician and the dog train hard together for seventeen weeks before going on the job.

Belgian Malinois canines are trained to sniff cars to detect bomb-related substances. If the dog senses something, it calmly sits down at the spot of detection to alert the technician. Even Secret Service vehicles are checked. "We don't take anything for granted," said one technician. "If a Secret Service vehicle is entering a secure area, we will have a dog check it out before it enters. If the vehicle was not in a secure location, we can't guarantee it is threat-free." The dog's nose is twenty times more sensitive than a human's.

Above: Countersniper teams are composed of highly qualified rifle sharpshooters who assist in providing a secure environment for protectees through superior vantage points. They are trained not to repel a potentially massive coordinated assault but to take out an individual assassin. The precision is necessary so that the sniper can hit the target in the middle of a crowd.

Countersnipers in the National Cathedral are observing a crowd during a presidential event.

These uniformed officers are pinned against a wall by hostile fire, and smoke is added to create a more realistic scenario.

Officers respond using automatic weapons during an exercise. The red band on the muzzle and magazine indicate the weapon has been modified to fire blank ammunition.

The personnel on the indoor range are using live fire for qualification.

This sequence of photos shows a simulated attack and a three-member Emergency Response Team preparing to repulse the assault. Note the red bands on the weapons indicating they are firing blanks.

Immobilizing and bringing a suspect into compliance as quickly as possible will prevent him from doing harm to innocent civilians. Trainees learn control techniques in daylight and nighttime situations.

Uniformed officers train to subdue a suspect without injury to themselves and, if possible, to the suspect.

The career path for a uniformed officer is officer, sergeant, lieutenant, captain, deputy chief, assistant chief, and chief. Officer technician and sergeant technician are specialized job titles.

Uniformed officers come from every state in the union and, if hired, must agree to reside in or near Washington, D.C., as a condition of employment. On their nametags is the state from which they hail.

The simulations are made as real as possible by using flash-bang grenades, other distraction devices, and smoke.

The Crime Scene Search Unit photographs, collects, and processes physical evidence and latent evidence. This unit of the Uniformed Division also prepares items and evidence for presentation in court. The Crime Scene Search Unit responds to all crime scenes at Secret Service–protected venues. It utilizes state-of-the-art equipment, and its technicians are highly trained and serve as expert witnesses in court.

The Emergency Response Team (ERT) provides an immediate and coordinated tactical response in and around Secret Service–protected facilities. *Department of Defense*

In the 1980s, the Secret Service created a specialized unit within the Uniformed Division called the Emergency Response Team (ERT) to provide an immediate response to emergencies at the White House complex and at foreign missions. ERT was formally established in 1985 as a specific response entity. Prior to 1985, a controlled response consisted of ad hoc Uniformed Division officers in response mode during their down time between assignments. ERT further evolved into a more defined unit in 1992 with a two-week formalized training program.

The Emergency Response Team deters or neutralizes the threat posed by organized groups or individuals.
Department of Defense

This indoor raid involves the use of tear gas, an immobilizing device to prevent harm to both the raid squad and the suspects.

Trainees, current Special Agents, and uniformed officers get plenty of mat time to ensure they stay in top physical condition.

Left: Five months after 9/11, the 2002 Winter Olympics opened in Salt Lake City, Utah. Throughout the Olympics, the Secret Service deployed its personnel in obvious ways. Its secret counterassault teams (CAT) were rarely seen but present. The CAT squad's job is to repel a coordinated terrorist attack. The Special Agent is holding a case, which probably contains a large automatic weapon.

Right: At the Winter Olympics, the Secret Service was responsible for protecting a nine-hundred-square-mile area in potentially frigid conditions, so agents were issued insulated yellow parkas to keep them warm. During the Olympic Games, an estimated eighty thousand people a day were crowding into venues to watch the competition. Another estimated three billion worldwide watched on TV. Protecting the athletes, spectators, and the games may have been the largest security operation in U.S. history. Moreover, this was not the only game the Secret Service attended. They also secured the Super Bowl in New Orleans just five days before the Olympics started.

Uniformed Division Bicycle Patrol Units cover areas that are difficult to patrol in a police vehicle or to adequately cover on foot. The units patrol areas around the perimeter of the White House, the vice president's residence, and foreign embassies in Washington, D.C.

In 1975, the duties of the Executive Protective Service (later renamed the Uniformed Division) were expanded to include protection of foreign diplomatic missions located throughout the United States and its territories.

The Uniformed Division's Ceremonial Honor Guard provides high-profile representation for the Secret Service at public and international agency ceremonies, law enforcement funerals, and other special events. Uniformed Division personnel appointed to the honor guard are trained for ceremonial duties, but remain assigned as operational members of the various Uniformed Division branches and are detailed for honor guard service as needed.

Above: Trainees will practice raids designed to simulate realism. The green spots on the body armor are hits from simunition.

Below: An unexpected attack on a Secret Service protectee is always a possibility, so agents will train in all conditions—rain, shine, daylight, and nighttime.

The Secret Service trains for any type of attack, from gas, as seen here, to heavy ordnance.

In 1921, John Larson built the first lie detector. It measured blood pressure and breathing. In 1930, Leonard Keeler added the measurement of galvanic skin resistance, thereby creating the modern polygraph machine. In 1930, Frye v. United States ruled polygraph tests are not acceptable as evidence in courts.

Trainees have to reach the top of the rope, ring the bell, and then climb back down the rope.

The Secret Service will use force when necessary to gain control or compliance of a suspect, and agents practice these techniques constantly.

The Secret Service pays a one-time stipend of $18,000 for a uniformed officer to move his or her household belongings to a residence near Washington, D.C.

The Secret Service has been charged by Congress with a number of little-known duties. They have guarded the precious metals in Treasury Department vaults. They have also guarded the most valuable historical documents of the United States: originals of the Constitution, the Declaration of Independence, the Gutenberg Bible, Lincoln's Second Inaugural Address, an American-owned copy of the Magna Carta, and more.

This is a simulated AOP in daylight. The Secret Service responds with overwhelming firepower to suppress the attack as quickly as possible.

The defensive training gets very physical, and trainees use protective gear to minimize injuries.

All Special Agents and uniformed officers learn first aid, emergency medical techniques, or become paramedics. Here, Special Agents are performing CPR on a mannequin of an infant. The open case is the first aid trauma (FAT) kit. It contains oxygen bottles, equipment, medicines to treat wounds and burns, splints for fractures, and other issues.

77

STUDENT VOLUNTEER SERVICE (INTERNSHIPS)

Working at U.S. Secret Service Headquarters in Washington, D.C., or in various field offices located throughout the United States will prepare a qualified student for a career with the U.S. Secret Service. The Student Intern Program provides unpaid, academically related work assignments that allow the student to explore career options as well as develop personal and professional skills. Students are expected to work a minimum of twelve hours per week, and not less than one semester, two quarters, or a summer session, and must be an undergraduate at the high-school, college, or university level. The program offers many advantages: career exploration early in a student's academic studies; exposure to new and emerging occupations and technologies; academic credit for the work performed (the academic institution determines the amount of credit); and work experience, which may be considered relevant if the student later applies for permanent employment in the Secret Service. The program, however, is not intended to provide the intern with investigative or protective experience.

Students must meet the following requirements in order to be considered for an intern position:
· Sixteen years of age at the time of appointment
· U.S. citizen
· Enrolled or accepted for enrollment during the upcoming semester or quarter as a full-time or part-time student in high school or in an educational institution not above the baccalaureate level
· Obtain an agreement from the educational institution to participate
· Not a son or daughter of a Secret Service employee
· Complete a preliminary background investigation and drug screening

Secret Service uniformed officers and officials assigned to the Office of Human Resources and Training have long served as firearms instructors and classroom instructors for the Secret Service. They are involved in all training programs at the JJRTC and at the Secret Service's post office range in Washington, D.C. Uniformed Division personnel are also involved in training Secret Service employees in many specialized skills, including protective operations driving, arrest techniques, defensive tactics, and the provision of medical care.

A Secret Service crime scene is sometimes better viewed from the air. If necessary, the Secret Service will make aerial photographs of a crime scene, and perhaps the photos will reveal evidence not obvious from the ground. Aircraft may also be used to survey a potential route for a motorcade and monitor an actual motorcade.
Henry M. Holden

continued from page 67

sophisticated equipment. They accomplish their protective mission by using observation, special sighting equipment, sophisticated weapons, and unique and superior vantage points. Often unseen, they are located on the roofs of strategic locations armed with a variety of weapons systems that can address individual ground threats. Their mission is to neutralize any long-range threat to a protectee. When the president is traveling outside the White House, the countersniper teams surveil the crowds through binoculars, night-vision scopes, and other devices.

While there have not been any incidents where a countersniper team has actually used its weapons, there may be occasional tense moments where the eyes of the countersnipers have prevented an incident and ensured the safety of a president or other protectee.

Since they will often be positioned at heights where they can overlook crowds or the protectee's safe movements, countersnipers must pass an acrophobia test (fear of heights). During the training, about half of all trainees will voluntarily remove themselves from the countersniper program, and others may be asked to reevaluate where else they may wish to work within the Secret Service.

Any previous experience with firearms is helpful, but Secret Service countersniper trainees will be taught to shoot all over again. One countersniper who was first exposed to the Secret Service as a marine guard at the White House said, "I learned to shoot in the Marine Corps, and it was helpful, but there was so much more to learn as a countersniper.

"If a person chooses not to go into the military, joining the Secret Service is another valid way to serve our country," he continued. "You get to serve on the front line in the war on terrorism, be in different environments, and at the same time, see the world."

As one twenty-year Uniformed Division supervisor said, "It's a unique job. No other law enforcement agency has the responsibil-ities that match the Secret Service. We get a chance to catch the bad guys and protect world leaders."

No one gets to view a presidential event without the Secret Service searching each individual for unauthorized material. This U.S. Army colonel is searched by a Secret Service Uniform Division officer as he disembarks the bus at the assembly area before the presidential inaugural parade. *Department of Defense*

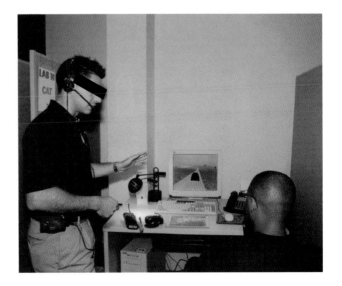

Computer-assisted learning and simulations make up a portion of all the training at the Beltsville field office.

FOUR

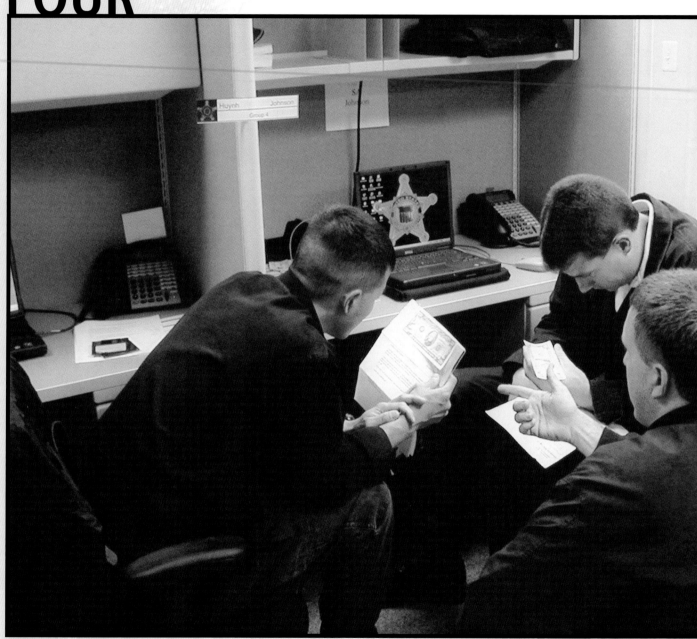

All Special Agents are trained to detect counterfeit currency. The Special Agents examining the counterfeit currency received thorough training in the Bureau of Engraving and Printing, but the bulk of the training is on the investigative side. The Secret Service says the percentage of counterfeit bills produced digitally has grown from one percent of bogus bills in 1995, before the last redesign, to forty percent in 2002.

Counterfeiting and Electronic Crime

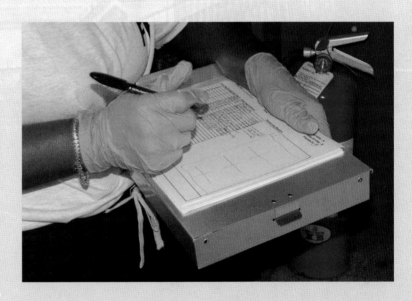

Technical Security Division (TSD) will photograph a crime scene and create a photo log, detailing the camera settings, the item photographed, who made the photograph, and more. *Henry M. Holden*

When the Secret Service was established after the Civil War, on July 5, 1865, about half of the U.S. money supply was fake. The Secret Service was therefore charged with suppressing counterfeiting and restoring public confidence in the currency. The work was so sensitive, its agents, or "operatives" as they were called, had their identities kept secret, thus creating a mystique of "secret agents."

Today, the primary investigative mission of the Secret Service is to safeguard the payment and financial systems of the United States. More than 140 years since its founding, over half of the Secret Service personnel investigate counterfeit and electronic fraud crimes. This is accomplished through the enforcement of the federal statutes to preserve the integrity of U.S. currency and financial obligations. Over the years, the Secret Service investigative responsibilities have expanded to include crimes involving computer and telecommunications fraud, identity theft, access device fraud, advance fee fraud, fraudulent electronic funds transfers, money laundering, and other technology-based crimes that have the potential to defraud and undermine American consumers, industries, and the economy. The Secret Service uses prevention-based training and methods to combat these crimes.

CRIMINAL INVESTIGATIVE DIVISION

The Criminal Investigative Division (CID) plans, reviews, and coordinates criminal investigations involving financial systems crimes. These include bank fraud, access device fraud, telemarketing, telecommunications fraud, computer fraud, automated payment systems and teller machines, direct deposit, investigations of forgery, counterfeiting, and more.

The secret of Secret Service protection is that it goes far beyond the business-suited bodyguards standing beside the president. The average person sees people with earpieces and sunglasses, but that is just the tip of the iceberg. Whether it is protecting the president, some other dignitary, a location, or an event, the Secret Service sets up layered defenses extending out from the protectee in both time and space, and relies on other agencies to assist in those defenses.

Manufacturing counterfeit U.S. currency or altering genuine currency to increase its value is a violation of Title 18, Section 471 of the U.S. Code and is punishable by a fine of up to $5,000, fifteen years' imprisonment, or both. Possession of counterfeit U.S. obligations with fraudulent intent is also a violation of the U.S. Code and is punishable by a fine, imprisonment for up to fifteen years, or both. Anyone who manufactures a counterfeit U.S. coin in any denomination above five cents is subject to the same penalties as all other counterfeiters. Anyone who alters a genuine coin to increase its numismatic or collector's value is in violation of the U.S. Code, which is punishable by a fine, imprisonment for up to five years, or both. Full-sized printed reproductions, including photographs of paper currency, checks, bonds, postage stamps, revenue stamps, and securities of the United States and foreign governments are violations punishable by a fine, imprisonment for up to fifteen years, or both.

At the close of the Civil War, between one-third and one-half of all U.S. paper currency in circulation was counterfeit. Hugh McCulloch, secretary of the Treasury appointed by President Abraham Lincoln, persuaded Lincoln to establish the Secret Service to fight counterfeiting. On April 14, 1865, just five days after the Civil War ended, Lincoln approved the plan. It was his last official act. Later that evening, John Wilkes Booth mortally wounded him. The U.S. Secret Service became an official government agency on July 5, 1865, when Chief William P. Wood was sworn in by Secretary Hugh McCulloch. In 1875, the first commission book and a new badge were issued to operatives.

COUNTERFEITING

There are only two criminal offenses specifically spelled out in the U.S. Constitution: treason and currency counterfeiting. Although the Secret Service protective details get most of the publicity, the service has never quit chasing counterfeiters.

Counterfeiting is one of the oldest crimes in history. It was a serious problem during the nineteenth century, when banks issued their own currency. At the beginning of the Civil War, there were approximately sixteen hundred state banks designing and printing their own notes. Each note carried a different design, making it difficult to distinguish the four thousand varieties of counterfeits from the seven thousand varieties of genuine notes.

The government hoped that with the adoption of a national currency in 1863, it would solve the counterfeiting problem. However, the national currency was soon counterfeited so extensively it became necessary for the government to take enforcement measures.

"Counterfeiting United States currency is now done on an international scale," said one supervising agent. The Treasury Department's Bureau of Engraving and Printing tries to outpace the counterfeiters by designing into the bills increasingly sophisticated security features, and issuing new bills every five to seven years to replace the worn currency.

"We have to keep abreast of the new technological advances; technology is driving the service today," he said. Today's counterfeiters use a wide range of readily available technologies—scanners, photocopiers, digital cameras, and plates etched with acid have replaced the old hand-engraving method. "Some of the computer-generated counterfeit notes are obvious to anyone who inspects their money," said one agent. "Here in the United States, we get more computer-generated notes, with twenties being the most common. Overseas countries generate more hundred-dollar bills. Most of those come from South America, [and] are smuggled in by couriers, known as 'mules,' in their luggage," he said.

In colonial times, the crime of counterfeiting was punishable by death.

As absurd as this fake $22 bill seems, it is illegal to make or sell such a note. The individual selling this note is pictured on the bill. He was selling them dressed as Uncle Sam on Fifth Avenue, across from St. Patrick's Cathedral, in New York City. *Henry M. Holden*

Rear side of the fake $22 bill. *Henry M. Holden*

In 2002, the U.S. Secret Service made 4,900 arrests for currency counterfeiting activities. The conviction rate for counterfeiting prosecutions is about ninety-nine percent.

In 1995, less than one percent of counterfeit notes detected in the United States were digitally produced. By 2002, that number had grown to nearly forty percent. In 2002, the U.S. Secret Service made 555 seizures of digital equipment, such as personal computers, involved in currency counterfeiting.

With electronic technologies widely available, quantities of counterfeit currency can be produced almost anywhere in the world. The equipment used by the casual counterfeiter and the career criminal is easily available in almost any city, and online. As technology becomes more advanced, lower prices make that equipment more affordable and more accessible.

All Special Agents are trained to detect counterfeit currency. They receive thorough training in the Bureau of Engraving and Printing, but the bulk of the training is on the investigative side. It is a painstaking process to track the bill back to its origin. "First, we try to interview the person who passed the bill," said one agent. "A lot of counterfeit bills show up in local neighborhoods, and often innocent persons pass them," she said.

To discover the source, an agent must first determine if the individual had criminal intent: in this case, knowingly passing a counterfeit bill. If there was no

Drugs and counterfeiting often go together and result in violent crimes that the Secret Service may investigate. This agent is preparing to photograph fingerprints at a crime scene. All Special Agents are trained in crime-scene photography and all the investigative duties of the Secret Service. *Henry M. Holden*

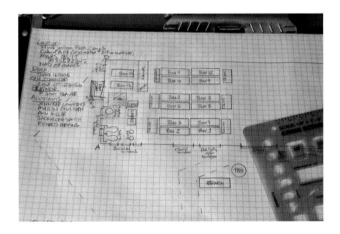

Every crime scene that the Secret Service investigates must be sketched out as part of the investigation. *Henry M. Holden*

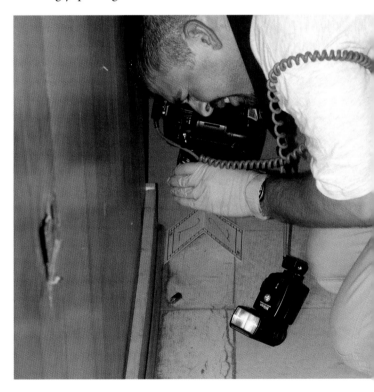

This Special Agent is photographing an ejected cartridge shell. If the weapon that ejected it is found, the Secret Service will be able to match the firing pin markings—minute marks made on the cartridge from the chamber and ejector—and positively connect the shell casing to the gun. *Henry M. Holden*

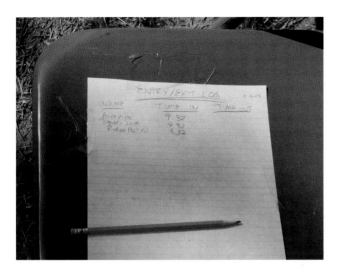

Only authorized TSD personnel would be permitted to access a crime scene, and they must account for their entry and departure from the scene. *Henry M. Holden*

Evidence, once recorded in the evidence log, must be packaged securely and labeled clearly. *Henry M. Holden*

The TSD does not rely on photography alone to record the evidence at a crime scene. Various hand-written logs such as an evidence log will also be kept. *Henry M. Holden*

Metal detectors are used to search for shell casings and other metallic evidence at a crime scene at a Secret Service–protected site. *Henry M. Holden*

Below: Identifying the precise location of the crime is important, especially if the case goes to trial. This handheld GPS-integrated radio has a built-in electronic compass to give a heading while the user is standing still and a barometric altimeter to provide extremely accurate elevation and pressure information that will assist users in identifying weather data. *Henry M. Holden*

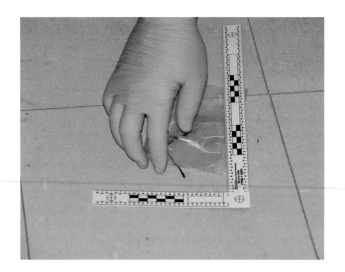

This fiber, found at a crime scene, has been bagged, tagged, and photographed alongside a comparison scale. Here, the technician is about to remove the evidence and package it for shipment back to the forensics lab. *Henry M. Holden*

Right: This cigarette, found at the crime scene, may reveal DNA evidence to the Secret Service forensic scientists. The DNA would then be entered in the Combined DNA Index System (CODIS) for possible identification. *Henry M. Holden*

criminal intent, the agent will attempt to backtrack to the previous source of the bills, perhaps a local merchant. "We will interview as many people as necessary to reach back and identify the source of the printing," she continued. "The public is the first line of defense in counterfeiting. The more public input we get, the closer we can get to shutting down a counterfeiting operation. The innocent individual gets hurt in this game," she said. "The person has to surrender the bill whether it is a twenty, or a hundred-dollar bill, and they do not get a real one in exchange."

Carpets will be vacuumed for trace evidence. The vacuum has a removable filter that will be packaged as evidence and sent to the lab, where a forensic scientist will examine it. *Henry M. Holden*

The Secret Service spends considerable time educating merchants on how to make sure the currency they take in is real. "Counterfeit currency is a real problem for the mom-and-pop store," said one agent. "If they accept a fake $100 bill, they can't exchange it for a real one, and they take a real loss."

In a small operation, counterfeit notes are often passed to the public one by one. Passers usually look for dimly lit, often busy environments, or holiday periods. They may pick a fast-food restaurant at noontime, or a movie premier, when the lines are long and the pressure is on to move the customers quickly. Unless it is a poorly counterfeited bill, the cashier will probably not pay much (if any) attention to the money. It is a quick exchange, and that is what the counterfeiter is counting on.

COMBATING COUNTERFEITING

To make counterfeiting more difficult, the money is not printed on a wood-based product, but one made of cotton fiber. The most recent bills contain new security threads and other features specifically designed to prevent color copying.

This Special Agent is examining documents that may be evidence in a crime. Any potential evidence must not be contaminated by fingerprints.

All Special Agents must have excellent interviewing skills.

The Secret Service responds to local police when the police believe the crime falls under the Secret Service's jurisdiction.

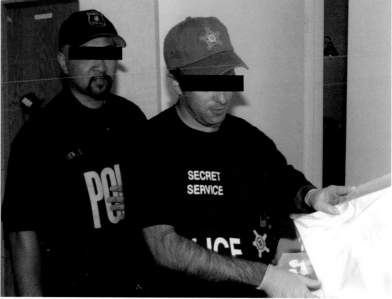

New, more sophisticated security features, however, do not deter some counterfeiters. Less than a month after the new $50 note was introduced, the Secret Service came across its first counterfeit $50 notes. "They weren't good reproductions," said one agent, "but they were good enough to pass at a local gas station."

The Secret Service uses modern techniques to stem the flow of counterfeit bills. In the Secret Service laboratories, technicians use special chemicals that react to traces of human perspiration that may reveal latent fingerprints on bills, but it still takes a trained agent to get to the source of the counterfeiting. Working undercover, Special Agents will seek to buy large blocks of counterfeit money and set up phony fencing operations in order to get to the origin of the bills, arrest the counterfeiters, and shut down the operation.

Recently, the Secret Service investigated more than fifty counterfeiting cases in several California cities during a holiday period, where counterfeit $100 bills were showing up. Fast food restaurants and small merchants accounted for many of the counterfeit purchases. "This happens because these criminals take advantage of the holidays and the rush of people," said one Special Agent. The Secret Service believes counterfeiters in Colombia produced the fake money. The counterfeit bills were printed on high-quality paper, but lacked most of the security features. They also had glaring errors and inaccuracies such as the words "USA 100" on Benjamin Franklin's jacket. This was a noticeable error, as the numeral 100 belongs in the bill's lower left corner.

A GLOBAL WAR ON COUNTERFEITING

The Secret Service is fighting the war against counterfeiting on a global scale. Counterfeiting is like a giant octopus whose tentacles stretch around the world. Everyday technology, such as scanners and color copiers, enables virtually anyone, anywhere to become a counterfeiter. However, foreign crime syndicates print much of the fake currency abroad, using traditional offset printing methods.

Some countries in South America, such as Ecuador, Guatemala, and El Salvador, have adopted the U.S. dollar as their own currency, and other countries are considering the move. According to government data, about sixty percent of the more than $650 billion of U.S. currency in circulation is abroad, and about $200 million dollars is probably counterfeit. However, the counterfeit currency today is far more difficult to trace than in the past.

The crime of counterfeiting coins and notes is as old as money itself and continues on a worldwide scale. Increasingly sophisticated security features and improved detection methods make the trade in counterfeiting more difficult, but the front line on the war against counterfeiting is at the cash register. The look and feel, the watermark, and the security threads are the most reliable ways of authenticating notes. *Henry M. Holden*

"The biggest problem continues to be counterfeit currency made in Colombia," said one agent. "The Colombian criminals have refined counterfeiting of U.S. currency to an art, and unless people examine bills closely, it is difficult to spot a fake."

"The same people who produce counterfeits that show up in Los Angeles produce the counterfeits that are showing up in Madrid, Spain, or Quito, Ecuador," said one agent.

It is well established that the international trade in counterfeit bills is linked to drug trafficking and arms trade, and the two combined sometimes lead to violent crimes that the Secret Service investigates. The number-one foreign source of counterfeits in Los Angeles comes from several countries in South America, where drug rings also flourish. Offset printers, for example, usually produce these counterfeits.

"Inkjet technology, off the desktop computer, seems to be more domestic," said the agent. "If we get offset notes, from traditional printing methods, it's likely coming from offshore."

With Latin American countries adopting the U.S. currency as their own, there is a likelihood for new illegal marketing opportunities for counterfeiting U.S. currency. If a financially corrupt government decided to produce U.S. currency notes to support its economy, it would be a major concern of the U.S. Secret Service.

NORTH HOLLYWOOD GANG
New York, Miami, and Los Angeles are hot spots for counterfeit activity in the United States. On average, the Secret Service detects $100,000 in counterfeit currency every week in the Los Angeles area. The Secret Service recently busted a counterfeit ring in North Hollywood that passed almost three-quarters of a million dollars in counterfeit currency to the public. The organizer was an individual with computer graphics skills and a Mac laptop.

"This person was about as good as they come in the reproduction of the new series of notes," said a Special Agent.

Chance favored the agents trying to shut the gang down when local police made a vehicle traffic stop. In the vehicle, they found, in plain sight, an envelope containing freshly printed $20 bills, with green ink still on the envelope.

Investigators can often determine the pecking order to the manufacturer of the bills by determining how much the person caught with the bills paid for the bills. The printer may sell the bills for ten cents on the dollar. If there are intermediaries in the chain, the price goes up each time the bills pass hands, until the person who actually passes the bill may have paid 50 cents, or more, on the dollar.

The driver, in this case, was a small player in a gang of more than two dozen, including the printer, middlemen, and the passers of the fake currency. "We traced the bills back to the gang's organizer, who was arrested in the process of printing more counterfeit bills," said one agent. "We always want to take the plant out."

ELECTRONIC CRIME

The Secret Service is one of the government's largest deterrents against computer crime. It has taken a lead role in the emerging area of cyber crime and, through a nationwide network of fifteen electronic crimes (or e-crimes) task forces, is working to reduce the financial toll e-crimes take on individuals and financial institutions.

As computers and related storage and communications devices increase in the United States, so does the likelihood of those devices being used in criminal activities. Criminals employ these technologies as a means of communication, as a tool for theft and extortion, and as a storage device to hide criminal evidence, illegal materials, or the fruits of a crime. In order to better fight

On June 4, 1980, Special Agents Julie Cross and Lloyd Bulman were conducting counterfeit surveillance in an area near the Los Angeles International Airport. Shortly after 9:00 p.m., two unknown males approached the agents' vehicle from the rear and shot both of them. Believing they were both dead, the assailants fled the scene. Agent Bulman, though stunned by the shotgun blast, was not seriously injured. Agent Cross died at the scene.

The evidence suggested the crime was an attempted robbery and not connected to the counterfeit investigation. The suspects took Agent Cross' handgun and a folding-stock Remington shotgun. For nine years the suspects remained unknown. The Secret Service continued its efforts to develop new leads in the case through a task force of its agents and members of the Los Angeles Police Department.

In 1989, the television show *Unsolved Mysteries* featured the Cross case. At that same time, a Los Angeles Police homicide detective arrested a suspect, Andre Alexander, for a triple murder that had occurred in 1978. Soon after his arrest, he became a prime suspect in the Cross investigation. In 1990, he was convicted of the triple murder and sentenced to life in prison without possibility of parole. Alexander was formally charged with Special Agent Cross' murder in 1992. In 1995, a jury found him guilty and sentenced him to death.

Machines at the twelve Federal Reserve banks, which collect cash from private banks, spot about twenty percent of seized counterfeit bills. The rest is caught or turned into the Secret Service by banks, individuals, or other law enforcement.

Thirty-nine percent of the fake currency in circulation in the United States was made using a computer.

Five African Americans have had their signatures on currency. Four of them were men: Blanche K. Bruce, Judson W. Lyons, William T. Vernon, and James C. Napier. They served as registers of the Treasury. Until the series 1923 currency, the two signatures on almost all currency (except fractional currency and demand notes) were of the treasurer and the register. The fifth African American whose signature appeared on currency was Azie Taylor Morton. She was the 36th treasurer of the United States and served from September 12, 1977, to January 20, 1981.

these crimes, the Secret Service must possess up-to-date knowledge and equipment to investigate these criminal activities effectively.

With technology advancing at seemingly Internet speed, staying ahead of the learning curve has become a major focus of the Secret Service. "As we've moved into the computer age, and specifically with the development of the Internet, we have become more active in [investigating] computer fraud," said one senior agent.

"Electronic crime, once thought to be the crime of the future, is becoming more prevalent," said one agent. "The reason why we are expanding the number of people we have and dedicating more personnel and training is because we see the future as happening now."

Secret Service electronic investigations have involved credit card fraud, unauthorized computer access, cellular and landline telephone service tampering, the production of false identification, threats made against the president, narcotics and illegal firearms trafficking, and even homicides. Computers are now used extensively in

A secure digital card is shown here. Because it is not much larger than a small postage stamp, it can be easily hidden and some can store up to one gigabyte of data that may contain evidence of a crime. *Henry M. Holden*

Jump drives, compact flash cards, and USB digital drives may be a source of evidence of an e-crime. If the perpetrator suspects the computer may be searched, he may remove the evidence from the desktop computer by transferring it to a portable storage device. *Henry M. Holden*

The second-largest operation in the Secret Service investigative function is forgery. Each year staggering sums of money are lost through forged checks and bonds. Until direct bank deposit became common, social security checks were the main target of forgery. The thieves would steal the checks from mailboxes and forge the signatures. More than 100,000 investigations of forged blank government checks and bonds consume the service each year.

Beginning in 1996, the government began adding advanced security features to the U.S. currency, the first major design change since 1928. Advanced copying technologies have raised the incidence of counterfeiting. Ink-jet printers, color copiers, and scanners are just a few of the tools criminals use to create bogus bills.

The Counterfeit Detection Act of 1992 permits color illustrations of U.S. currency provided: the illustration is of a size less than three-fourths or more than one and one-half, in linear dimension, of each part of the item illustrated; the illustration is one-sided; and all negatives, plates, positives, digitized storage media, graphic files, magnetic media, optical storage devices, and anything else used in the making of the illustration are destroyed and/or deleted or erased after their final use.

facilitating many crimes investigated by the Secret Service. However, computers also provide technical assistance to Special Agents in developing their cases, including the preparation and service of search warrants on electronic storage devices.

RECOGNIZING POTENTIAL EVIDENCE

Computers and digital media are now major tools and weapons involved in criminal activities. Special Agents are taught that a computer may be contraband, the spoils of the crime, a tool in committing the offense, or a storage

Cell phones, electronic paging devices, and computers equipped with wireless cards can be employed in e-crimes and may make the evidence more elusive. The cell phone user can e-mail the evidence to another cell phone, and the wireless computer can transmit the evidence to a remotely located device, perhaps another computer in the attic of the house. Potential evidence contained in wireless devices includes numbers called, numbers stored for speed dial, and caller ID for incoming calls. Other information contained in the memory of wireless telephones includes phone/pager numbers, names and addresses, personal identification numbers (PINs), voicemail access numbers and passwords, debit card numbers, calling card numbers, and e-mail and Internet access information. If it is necessary to access the device, all actions associated with the access should be noted in order to document the chain of custody to ensure its admission in court. *Henry M. Holden*

device holding evidence of a crime. The investigation of any criminal activity may produce electronic evidence. Computers and related evidence range from a large mainframe computer to a pocket-sized personal data assistant (PDA), a floppy diskette, CD, or the small, electronic chip devices such as jump drives and USB digital drives. Images, audio, text, and other data on these media are easily altered or destroyed, so the Secret Service learns to recognize, protect, seize, and search such devices using appropriate federal statutes, policies, and guidelines.

INSIDER THREATS

One potential method to damage the U.S. economy is through insider threats or actions against the financial community. These actions may result in a financial loss or monetary crisis in banks, credit unions, and other financial institutions. The Secret Service and the Computer Emergency Readiness Team Coordination Center (CERT CC) of Carnegie Mellon University are working to identify the data and the potentially vulnerable critical systems. They are also advising the institutions in the private industry, government, and law enforcement sectors on how to recognize the threats and guard and secure their networks against future threats. They are also finding ways to identify individuals who may pose a threat to those data and systems.

Right: Although data in a computer can be abstracted to a series of ones and zeros, the delete key does not simply delete the data that may contain evidence of a crime; it resides in the swap file. However, if the computer is switched on and used, new data replaces some of the old contents in the swap file. This presents the Special Agent with an interesting challenge: retrieve the old files without turning on the computer. Fortunately, there is equipment that can copy the contents of the hard drive without turning on the computer. Computer technicians will perform a bloodless surgery to reveal hidden evidence of a crime and possibly the fruits of the crime. Secret Service agents may examine, in a laboratory setting, any and all electronic data-processing and computer-storage devices, from central processing units and internal and peripheral storage devices, to software and programs used to communicate with other terminals, and any computer modems, monitors, printers, etc., that may have been used while engaging in specific illegal conduct, as defined in the appropriate federal statutes and warrants. *Henry M. Holden*

Most of the incidents the Secret Service and CERT have examined were technically undeveloped, straightforward, and involved the exploitation of nontechnical vulnerabilities such as business rules, rather than vulnerabilities in a network. For example, as part of their normal responsibilities, two credit union employees modified credit reports based on new, updated information the company received. In the fall of 1996, however, they misused their authorized access and

continued on page 96

Phishing is the act of sending an e-mail to a user falsely claiming to be an established legitimate enterprise in an attempt to defraud the user into surrendering private information that will be used for identity theft. The e-mail directs the user to visit a website where they are asked to update personal information, such as passwords and credit card, social security, and bank account numbers—information that the legitimate organization already has. The bogus website is set up only to steal the user's information. In 2004, phishing swindles cost banks and credit card issuers more than $1.2 billion.

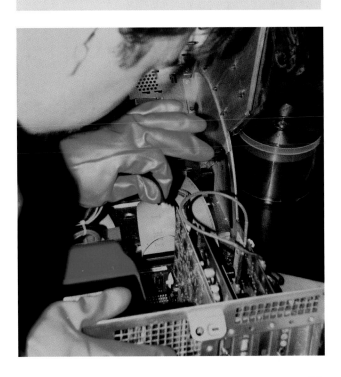

In one fiscal year, the Secret Service opened 2,467 cases, closed 2,963 cases, and arrested 2,429 individuals for access device fraud.

The Secret Service, best known for protecting presidents, has been helping the National Center for Missing and Exploited Children since 1994, when Congress expanded the Service's mission. Many missing and exploited children met their assailants on a computer. The agency has aided over 700 child abuse, abduction, and homicide probes, including a 1997 case in which a nine-year-old girl was left for dead in a housing project after being sexually assaulted, beaten, and poisoned. She survived, but was paralyzed, blind, and unable to speak. Secret Service forensic experts matched writing carved into the girl's abdomen with the handwriting of a suspect. The suspect was sentenced to 120 years in prison on multiple counts of criminal sexual assault, aggravated kidnapping, and attempted murder.
Henry M. Holden

Right: The Integrated Automated Fingerprint Identification System (IAFIS) is the largest network of its kind and is composed of remote latent fingerprint terminals providing a connection to fingerprint databases with access to more than 30 million fingerprints. This enables the fingerprint specialist to digitize a single latent fingerprint from an item of evidence and to search for its likeness from fingerprint databases throughout the country. Trained human eyes are usually needed to verify or make a match. Potential matches are limited to those that already exist in a database.

On October 26, 2004, in an action called Operation Firewall, Secret Service agents, along with local and overseas law enforcement, shut down Shadowcrew.com with simultaneous raids in the United States, Europe, and South America. Operation Firewall began in July 2003 as an investigation into access device fraud. The case evolved into a highly technical, transnational investigation involving global credit card fraud and identity theft over the Internet. Beginning in early 2004, data obtained through court-authorized intercepts revealed internal communications, transactions, and practices of Shadowcrew.com and other criminal organizations. The amount of information gathered during the investigation is approximately two terabytes—the equivalent of an entire university's academic library. During the previous two years, online groups called Shadowcrew, Carderplanet, and Darkprofits had sold at least 1.7 million valid but stolen credit card numbers, 18 million e-mail accounts, and scores of identification documents—everything from passports to driver's licenses to student IDs—on the Internet. Estimated losses to merchants and banks from Shadowcrew activities totaled more than $4 million. Operation Firewall led to the arrest of suspects in eight states and six foreign countries. The indictment of nineteen Shadowcrew founders, moderators, and members for trafficking in stolen identity information, documents, and credit and debit card numbers followed.

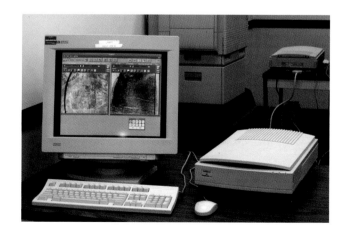

Discovery of electronic evidence can lead to the identification of a criminal. Computers are used extensively in facilitating many crimes investigated by the Secret Service, and they can be the source of evidence of a crime. The Secret Service trains its personnel to recognize, protect, seize, and search such devices using the Fourth Amendment of the Constitution, appropriate federal statutes, policies, and guidelines. Special Agents may ask the following four questions to determine the role of the computer in the crime: Is the computer contraband or fruits of a crime? For example, was the computer software or the computer itself stolen? Was the computer system a tool used in the offense? For example, was the system actively used by the defendant to commit the offense, or were fake IDs or other counterfeit documents prepared using the computer, scanner, or color printer? Was the computer system only incidental to the offense, which means being used to store evidence of the offense? For example, was a drug dealer maintaining his inventory and sales records in his computer? Finally, was the computer system both instrumental to the offense and a storage device for evidence? For example, did the computer hacker use the computer to attack other systems and also use it to store stolen records? *Henry M. Holden*

Fingerprints are unique patterns created by skin ridges found on the palm side of fingers and thumbs. Fingerprints are defined by patterns of loops, whirls, and arches. This fingerprint examiner is comparing a latent fingerprint to an inked fingerprint. A variety of techniques, including use of chemicals, powders, lasers, alternate light sources, and reflective ultraviolet imaging source (RUVIS), use intensified UV reflectance instead of fluorescence, as in forensic light sources.

In 1997, juveniles hacked into a major telephone company's computer switch and disrupted radar and runway control at a busy airport in Massachusetts. Area 911 emergency telephone service was also affected. The investigation and computer data analysis revealed the same vulnerability existed in 22,000 telephone company switches across the country. The systems also affected major financial institutions, coast guard operations, and heart-monitoring networks' communications. The Secret Service made arrests, and vulnerable equipment was replaced.

Chemical fuming is one of several methods used to unmask latent prints.

Another method of unmasking fingerprints is dusting.

continued from page 93

removed negative credit indicators in some records. They also added false positive credit indicators to selected credit histories in exchange for money. Their criminal actions caused the company more than $251,000 in fraud losses.

In another instance, an employee who had recently quit a company in a dispute over a salary issue planted a "logic bomb" in the company's computer. A logic bomb is a slightly more sophisticated approach than the previous example. It is potentially more damaging, since it is a malevolent code imbedded in a computer system and configured to execute at a specific time or on a specific system command, such as the execution of a utility program. This logic bomb deleted 10 billion files in the computer systems of an international financial services company. It cost the company more than $3 million to repair the damage.

IDENTITY CRIME

Identity theft has become a major issue among residents in the United States and a focus of the Secret Service. "Identity crime is not directed at any particular individual or demographic," said one agent, "Instead, it affects all

In 1995, the New York Electronic Crimes Task Force (NYECTF), a division of the U.S. Secret Service, was developed specifically to help companies improve their cyber security. It worked so well in New York that the Patriot Act called for the Secret Service to establish similar groups across the nation to prevent electronic crime.

Because computers are a source of both investigative leads and evidentiary material, the Secret Service has established the Electronic Crimes Special Agent Program (ECSAP), which trains agents to conduct forensic examinations of computers that were used in criminal activities. Once trained, these agents can preserve any investigative leads within the computer as well as any evidence needed for subsequent prosecutions.

The Secret Service often cooperates with other law enforcement personnel.

The Fourth Amendment states, "The right of the people to be secure in their persons, houses, papers, and effects, against unreasonable searches and seizures, shall not be violated, and no warrants shall issue, but upon probable cause . . ." This amendment applies to all electronic storage devices. The Secret Service needs search warrants to gather evidence. If the evidence recovered at a crime scene implicates an individual, the warrant must state the probable cause for the search, specify that the item(s) that the warrant covers is part of the crime, and state where it may be found. (There is generally also a time frame placed on the warrant.) There are exceptions to the necessity of obtaining a search warrant. A person can grant consent to search his or her property. There may be exigent circumstances that require some kind of probable cause. An emergency may make obtaining the warrant impractical, useless, dangerous to the officers or others, or unnecessary, or may result in the physical destruction of the evidence. The threat or harm must be imminent, not just a possibility.

The center of the universe for the Secret Service Electronic Crimes Task Force was 7 World Trade Center, which stood near the North Tower. Inside the 47-story building was the Secret Service's largest field office, with more than 200 employees. On September 11, 2001, all escaped except Master Special Officer Craig Miller, who perished in the collapse of the tower when the building was reduced to rubble.

Most of the Special Agents walked out of the building with their gun and a handheld radio. All the evidence stored at 7 World Trade Center went down with the building. They lost their network, their computers, and all the equipment they used. Five years of work, 800 convictions, and 85,000 square feet of space—gone.

One Special Agent had a personal data assistant (PDA) in his pocket. It was the only record they had of their contacts in law enforcement and their industry partners. More than fifty law enforcement agencies, 200 corporations, and twelve universities donated tens of thousands of dollars in equipment and hundreds of volunteer hours to enable the Secret Service's New York field office to become operational at John Jay College within forty-eight hours of the attacks.

This computer chip may have a cache of information that becomes evidence in a criminal proceeding.

Henry M. Holden

Under Title 18, Section 1029 of the U.S. Code, the Secret Service is the primary federal agency tasked with investigating access device fraud and its related activities. This law also applies to crimes involving access device numbers such as debit cards, automated teller machine (ATM) cards, computer passwords, personal identification numbers (PINs) used to activate ATMs, credit card or debit card account numbers, long-distance access codes, and the computer chips in cellular phones that assign billing.

INSIDER THREATS

In eighty-seven percent of the cases studied, the insiders employed simple, legitimate user commands to carry out their illegal activities. In seventy percent of cases, the insiders exploited or attempted to exploit systemic vulnerabilities in applications and/or processes or procedures (e.g., business rule checks, authorized overrides) to carry out the illegal activity. In sixty-one percent of the cases, the insiders exploited vulnerabilities inherent in the design of the hardware, software, or network.

Americans, regardless of age, gender, nationality, or race." Victims can include office workers, factory workers, police officers, corporate and government executives, celebrities, and all ranks of military personnel.

HOW IDENTITY THEFT OCCURS

"Skilled identity thieves use a variety of methods to gain access to personal information," said one agent. "They mine information from business records by stealing records, such as social security numbers, from an employer. They may bribe an employee who has access to these records, or they hack into the company's computers. They search through trash or dumps in a practice called

GUARDING AGAINST INSIDER THREATS

· A negative, work-related event triggers most insider crimes.

· Most of the insiders had acted out in an inappropriate manner in the workplace before committing the crime.

· The majority of insiders planned their activities in advance.

· When hired, the majority of insiders were granted system administrator or privileged access, but less than half of all of the insiders had authorized access at the time of the incident.

· Insiders used unsophisticated methods for exploiting systemic vulnerabilities in applications, processes, and/or procedures, but relatively sophisticated attack tools were also employed.

· The majority of insiders compromised computer accounts, created unauthorized back door accounts, or used shared accounts in their attacks.

· Remote access was used to carry out the majority of the attacks.

· The majority of the insider attacks were only detected once there was a noticeable irregularity in the information system or a system became unavailable.

· Insider activities caused organizations financial losses, negative impacts to their business operations, and damage to their reputations.

'dumpster diving.' Others may obtain credit reports by abusing their employer's authorized access to credit reports. They steal mail, including bank and credit card statements, preapproved credit offers, new checks, or tax information. They steal personal information from a victim's home and trash. What the victims have in common is the difficult, time-consuming, and potentially expensive task of repairing the damage that has been done to their credit, their savings, and their reputations," he said.

In the world of computer forensics, the word "computer" extends beyond desktops, laptops, and pocket computers. It applies to any device containing a microprocessor. Cameras, video recorders, pagers, and more contain chips to process and store data records. Other such devices include numeric pagers (receive only numeric digits; can be used to communicate numbers and code); alphanumeric pagers (receive numbers and letters and can carry full text); voice pagers (can transmit voice communications, sometimes in addition to alphanumeric); and two-way pagers (containing incoming and outgoing messages). To safely and legally seize this potential evidence, the agent should turn off the pager once it is no longer in proximity to the suspect. Continued access to electronic communication over a pager without proper authorization may be construed as unlawful interception of electronic communication.
Henry M. Holden

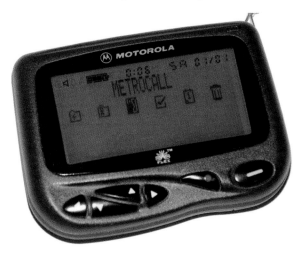

OPERATION MAGSTRIPE

A 2004 survey conducted among security and law enforcement executives by CSO magazine, in cooperation with the Secret Service and Carnegie Mellon University's CERT Coordination Center, found more organizations reporting an increase in electronic crimes and network, system, or data intrusions. Forty-three percent reported an increase in e-crimes and intrusions. The previous year, seventy percent reported at least one e-crime or intrusion against their organizations. Respondents say that e-crime cost their organizations approximately $666 million in 2003. Fifty-six percent of respondents reported operational losses, twenty-five percent stated financial losses, and twelve percent declared other types of losses.

E-CRIMES IMPACT

A 2004 survey conducted among security and law enforcement executives by CSO magazine, in cooperation with the Secret Service and Carnegie Mellon University's CERT Coordination Center, found more organizations reporting an increase in electronic crimes and network, system, or data intrusions. Forty-three percent reported an increase in e-crimes and intrusions. The previous year, seventy percent reported at least one e-crime or intrusion against their organizations. Respondents say that e-crime cost their organizations approximately $666 million in 2003. Fifty-six percent of respondents reported operational losses, twenty-five percent stated financial losses, and twelve percent declared other types of losses.

FIVE

During a presidential event, the Secret Service will monitor broadcast news stations and videos from cameras in helicopters along the parade route, and even in a subway system. Specialists in chemical, biological, and radiological terrorism will mingle with the crowd.

Threat Assessment

President Bush deplanes at Andrews Air Force Base on September 11, 2001, after arriving from Offutt Air Force Base, Nebraska. Even on the secure Air Force base, Secret Service agents are close by. *U.S. Air Force*

The Secret Service has to plan and prepare for any event—the lone assassin or an organized plot by a group. Today, the protection aspect of the Secret Service has taken on a more urgent tone because of the global aspects of terrorism and the array of weapons available to potential assassins. In the past, attempts on the lives of U.S. presidents have been from lone assassins, and the specter of a lone assassin breaching security and getting close to the president still remains a constant concern. However, the global threats are escalating almost daily in technological sophistication in the shape of nerve gas, dirty bombs, biological agents, and shoulder-fired weapons, to name a few.

While the Special Agent and uniformed officer are an obvious part of every protective effort, they are backed up by a large team of specialists, seldom seen or heard. They are part of the threat assessment and risk analysis that are part of the protective duties of the Secret Service. The formulation and analysis of data and intelligence to establish a framework for developing the protective effort is a massive undertaking. It is a federal crime to threaten the president, and all telephone threats, collected from the White House, local police, and the radio and television stations, are reviewed. While the service will not discuss the threats, as it may give encouragement to others, they take every threat seriously, and they investigate every threat. "Unless you're paranoid,

Around 700 A.D., the Chinese used fingerprints to establish the identity the originators of documents and clay sculpture, but without any formal classification system. Today, fingerprint technology is still a major investigative tool of the Secret Service.

In Roy v. United States (1969), the court dealt expressly with the issue of intent and held: "The statute to require only that the defendant intentionally make a statement, written or oral, in a context, or under such circumstances, wherein a reasonable person would foresee that the statement would be interpreted by those to whom the maker communicates the statement as a serious expression of an intention to inflict bodily harm upon or take the life of the president, and that the statement not be the result of mistake, duress, or coercion."

In recent years, the Service realized that the threat of an attack on a protectee or protective site using chemical, biological, or radiological materials has become significant.

Whether it is a drill or a real attack, the Secret Service must be prepared to take immediate action.

The U.S. Secret Service New York field office, located in 7 World Trade Center, was destroyed on September 11, 2001, as a result of the terrorist attacks. Throughout the day of the attacks and subsequently, Secret Service agents continually and knowingly placed themselves in exceptional danger in their efforts to save lives. Master Special Officer Craig Miller was the only Secret Service employee lost on that day. *Department of Defense*

In 1856, Sir William Herschel, a British officer working for the Indian Civil Service, began to use thumbprints on documents both as a substitute for written signatures for illiterates and to verify document signatures.

Of the individuals who come to the Secret Service's attention as creating a possible danger to one of its protectees, approximately seventy-five percent are mentally ill. The Secret Service is particularly concerned that media attention given to cases involving threats against protectees may provoke violent acts from such mentally unstable persons.

In 1867, Secret Service responsibilities were broadened to include detecting persons perpetrating frauds against the government. This later resulted in investigations into the Ku Klux Klan, illegal distillers, smugglers, mail robbers, land frauds, and a number of other violations of the federal laws.

WHAT CONSTITUTES A "THREAT"?

In 1917, Congress authorized permanent protection of the president's immediate family and made "threats" directed toward the president a federal violation. According to U.S. Code 18 Section 871, "Whoever knowingly and willfully deposits for conveyance in the mail or for a delivery from any post office or by any letter carrier any letter, paper, writing, print, missive, or document containing any threat to take the life of, to kidnap, or to inflict bodily harm upon the president of the United States . . . or other officer next in the order of succession to the office of president of the United States, . . . or knowingly and willfully otherwise makes any such threat against the president, president-elect, vice president or other officer next in the order of succession to the office of president, . . . shall be fined under this title or imprisoned not more than five years, or both."

The mascot of the Technical Security Division (TSD) is able to juggle many technologies at the same time. *Henry M. Holden*

you're not successful," said one agent. "There are regular daily threats. History has shown that someone has always wanted to kill a president."

THE FORENSIC SERVICES DIVISION

The Forensic Services Division (FSD) has the most up-to-date equipment to accomplish the threat-assessment mission. Scientists, electronics and computer specialists, and other professionals examine and evaluate the daily inflow of threatening letters and phone calls, as well as suspicious mail.

FSD also uses a Voice Identification Program that deals with the science of forensic phonetics—the analysis of speech recordings. All threats are analyzed and compared to the database of previous threat calls. In some cases, if the caller's identity is known, the Secret Service may interview the person to determine if the individual is in a rational, confused, or mentally disturbed state. The Secret Service must try to differentiate between those who make threats and those who have the capacity to carry them out, such as persons with access to weapons.

INTENT TO CARRY OUT THREATS AGAINST SECRET SERVICE PROTECTEES

The First Amendment states: "Congress shall make no law respecting an establishment of religion, or prohibiting the free exercise thereof, or abridging the freedom of speech." Courts have ruled that proof that threatening words uttered in a context such that a reasonable person would interpret them as mere political hyperbole, idle talk, or jest, indicates that the words do not constitute a threat within the scope of the statute. However, the actual intent to carry out a threat is not a requisite to violation of the statute.

In the late nineteenth century, the Secret Service thwarted a plot to kidnap the body of the late President Abraham Lincoln and hold it for ransom.

The Forensic Information System for Handwriting (FISH), a national database of threat letters, allows a document examiner to scan and digitize text and handwritings, and later search and compare that material against previously recorded documents. Virtually every letter has some traceable clue. An individual's handwriting is unique, personal, and often hard to disguise. For handwritten letters, technicians can trace the papers, the chemical composition of the inks, and the handwriting styles back to the people who use them. With chemical baths and other technologies, they have the ability to lift latent finger, palm, foot, and toe prints, even remnants of DNA from dandruff or other skin particles. Clues on the paper, grease or oils, and writing or printing styles may help document examiners identify a suspect if he or she is in the database. The clues will be combined to provide a profile of the suspect.

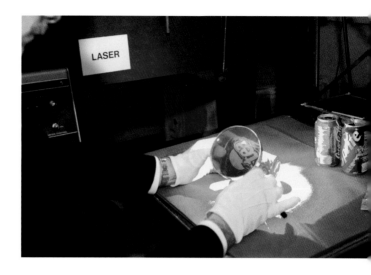
The TSD often will use artificial and alternate light sources to reveal clues and evidence of a crime.

During World War II, the Secret Service protected the Gutenberg Bible, Declaration of Independence, and the Magna Carta. It also had to deal with counterfeit ration coupons, war bonds, and whiskey stamps.

CONDITIONAL THREAT TO SECRET SERVICE PROTECTEES

The courts have ruled that the use of conditional language is pertinent in evaluating the "threat" content of a statement. Such evaluation must take the full context of an alleged threat into consideration. In Alexander v. United States (1969), the courts ruled: "Motive of the defendant may well be relevant to the inquiry. Other factors for consideration would include such matters as audience reaction, intoxication, a history of mental illness unaccompanied by dangerous propensities, and capability of, or preparations by the defendant to act upon his/her words. If a prospective defendant's conduct reasonably appears to amount to a serious expression of intent to inflict harm, action to prosecute should follow immediately."

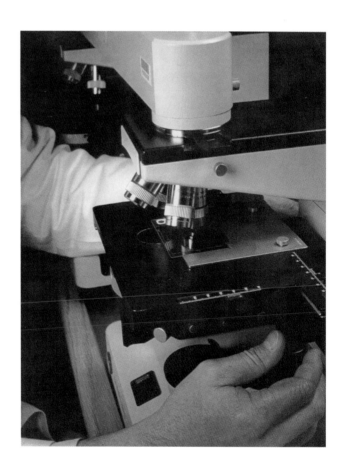
The microscope is one of the oldest and most reliable instruments used to see what is often beyond the human eye, and just one tool in the TSD toolbox.

The Secret Service has the largest database of paper specimens in the world. It can determine how the paper was processed, what type of tree the paper came from, and where and when the paper was made, and

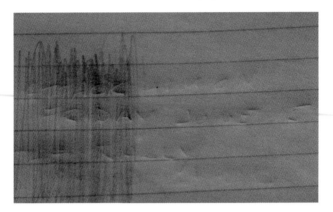

The Questioned Documents Unit will take a page with an impression from a previous page and unmask the writing, and possibly clues to pursue. *Henry M. Holden*

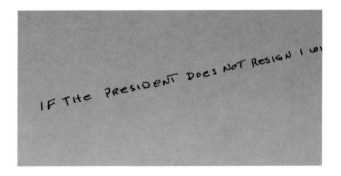

The Secret Service investigates every threat letter it receives. This letter has an obvious idiosyncrasy that may lead investigators to its author. Writing habits learned in school are difficult to change—the way of holding a pen, shaping the letters, and spacing the words and lines. These and other persistent qualities make handwriting a useful tool in analyzing a document. Secret Service document examiners will look for certain characteristics—distinctive letter formations such as the direction of letter strokes, and conventional letter and word construction—on the questioned document and attempt to find a match in their database. While this note is in uppercase letters, the letter e is consistently in lowercase, and the loop bisects the curved portion of the letter. *Henry M. Holden*

possibly sold. These clues may lead investigators to a suspect. This system is now available to federal, state, and local investigators in the investigations of threats against public officials, as well as cases involving missing and sexually exploited children.

The Instrument Analysis Services Section houses the International Ink Library, the most complete forensic collection of writing inks worldwide. It contains over eight thousand samples. This collection is used to identify the source of suspect writing by not only providing the type and brand of writing instrument, but the earliest possible date that a document could have been produced. This section also maintains a watermark collection of over twenty-two thousand images as well as collections of plastics, toners, and computer printer inks.

FSD also accesses the Integrated Automated Fingerprint Identification System (IAFIS). This network is

In 2002, the Department of Homeland Security was established. The Secret Service was transferred from the Department of the Treasury to the new department effective March 1, 2003.

The electrostatic dust-print lifter is a device that deploys an electrostatic field on a Mylar film to lift dust prints from various surface types.

In 1994, Congress ordered the Secret Service to assist in finding missing children by using its excellent forensics lab to identify fingerprints, handwriting on ransom notes, trace evidence, and more. Recently, it has been called on to do assessments of school shootings and security at several state capitols and airports.

the largest of its kind and is composed of remote latent-fingerprint terminals providing access to databases with more than 47 million sets of fingerprints. This enables the fingerprint specialist to digitize a single latent fingerprint from an item of evidence and to search for its likeness from fingerprint databases throughout the country. These findings often provide the investigator with a suspect's name.

Forensic examiners in FSD provide analysis for questioned documents, false identification, credit cards, and other related forensic science areas. The division coordinates photographic, graphic, video, audio, and image enhancement services. In addition, FSD is responsible for handling the Forensic Hypnosis Program. Forensic hypnosis is used to enhance or probe the memory or recall of an individual for information in a criminal case. Forensic hypnosis places a person in a trancelike state that may resemble sleep, but is instead an altered state of consciousness more akin to a lucid dream. While the individual is in a trance he or she is alert, but focused in a way that differs from the normal conscious state. Much of the forensic assistance the Secret Service offers is unique technology operated in this country only by FSD.

FSD also manages the Secret Service's polygraph program nationwide. The Polygraph Examination Program is known as a forerunner in the law enforcement community for advancing the art of physiologically detecting deception. Polygraph examinations are a major

All Secret Service employees must have a top-secret clearance. This clearance applies to information or material the unauthorized disclosure of which could reasonably be expected to cause exceptionally grave damage to the national security. In addition, some classified information is so sensitive that even the extra protection measures applied to top-secret information are not sufficient. Additional categories called "special access programs" are used to protect presidential, military, intelligence, antiterrorism, and other sensitive activities.

Special access programs are regulated by statute, and are defined as deliberately designated programs where need-to-know or access controls beyond those normally provided to classified information are created. Compartmented programs cover such sensitive areas as the continuity of government and presidential communications. One classification is sensitive compartmented information (SCI). Each category of SCI is represented by a distinct code word, and these code words are further divided into various compartments. To have access to classified information, one must possess the necessary two elements: a level of security clearance at least equal to the classification of the information and the need to know the information in order to perform one's duties.

The forensic hypnotist must be proficient in the history of hypnosis, induction techniques, deepening techniques, and emerging the witness/victim. The forensic hypnotist must also be prepared to have his or her total background, statements, and all credentials examined in minute detail.

INTEGRATED AUTOMATED FINGERPRINT IDENTIFICATION SYSTEM (IAFIS)

The IAFIS is a national fingerprint and criminal-history system. The IAFIS provides automated fingerprint search capabilities, latent searching capability, electronic image storage, and electronic exchange of fingerprints and responses, twenty-four hours a day, 365 days a year. As a result of submitting fingerprints electronically, agencies receive electronic responses to the best ten criminal matches within two hours.

The IAFIS maintains the largest biometric database in the world, containing the fingerprints and corresponding criminal history information for more than 47 million subjects in the Criminal Master File. The fingerprints and corresponding criminal history information are submitted voluntarily by state, local, and federal law enforcement agencies.

TSD team will survey railroad routes, waterways, ports, and highways, looking for potential hazards and to prevent accidents such as the 1984 Bhopal, India, incident where the accidental release of methyl isocyante killed over 4,000 persons and left another 2,700 permanently disabled.

The Secret Service appoints all new physical security specialists to the Washington, D.C., area. Generally, physical security specialists experience frequent travel,

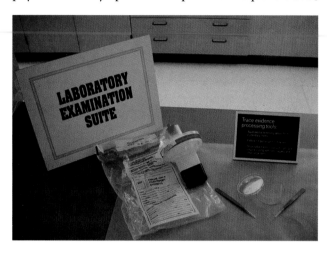

HAMMER members may be called upon to sample trace evidence and transport it to a lab for analysis. The kit includes spatulas for removing debris from evidence, a pillbox for preserving the debris, and a disposable vacuum canister for processing vehicles, carpets, and other large items.

Members of HAMMER must be aware of chemical, biological, and radiological detection and countermeasures, and know how to use the array of protective clothing available.

shift work, and possible reassignments to other Secret Service offices in the United States. A PSS may spend twenty years or more in any of the fourteen field offices and may experience a change in duty station every four to seven years, depending on the needs of the Secret Service. A physical security specialist usually spends at least five years in a protective advance team before qualifying for a lead position.

HAZARDOUS AGENT MITIGATION MEDICAL EMERGENCY RESPONSE

In response to certain potential threats, the Technical Security Division created a special unit called the Hazardous Agent Mitigation Medical Emergency Response (HAMMER) team. HAMMER is deployed on a case-by-case basis, with the emphasis on prevention through deterrence.

The HAMMER team may be composed of several PSS, Uniformed Division officers, or Special Agents with skills that complement the team. They are responsible for providing immediate support to the protective detail. Their single goal is to protect the president and anyone under Secret Service protection. The HAMMER team provides the protective detail with equipment, rapid intervention, communication, and medical support. It has the capability to identify hazardous agents, decontaminate, and evacuate the protectee(s). In addition, it may provide support for other first responders, and take environmental or other samplings for lab analysis. The

The HAMMER team is also capable of providing a variety of non-chemical- and biological-related duties, such as basic vehicle extrication, elevator rescue, forcible entry, and other emergency situations, and they will plan and coordinate any needed responses with local fire departments.

team operates from custom-designed rescue vehicles, and responds at the direction of a team leader who, for command purposes, remains in proximity to the protectee, but outside the potential contamination zone.

The HAMMER team's standard apparatus includes decontamination equipment, field identification systems, sampling units, patient treatment and transport devices, forcible-entry tools, rope-rescue apparatus, life-support systems, winch systems, and other rescue tools.

The team is capable of providing a variety of duties not related to chemical and biological threats, such as basic vehicle extrication, elevator rescue, forcible entry, and other emergency responses. They will also plan

Eighty percent of Technical Security Division (TSD) personnel have former military explosive, chemical, or Special Forces backgrounds. The remainder comes from civilian backgrounds of fire, hazardous material, EMS, or chemical expertise.

President Lyndon Johnson addresses a crowd while standing on the back of a limousine in May 1964. The Secret Service agent is holding the president's hand to steady him and, if necessary, pull him to safety. Remarkably, the president was still using an open-top limousine after the Kennedy assassination. President Ronald Reagan was the last president to ride in an open car in a public motorcade. *Library of Congress*

FIELD-EXPEDIENT GASEOUS DECONTAMINATION PROCEDURES

· Evacuate area
· Flush/decontaminate face with water or prepackaged decontamination materials
· Don mask
· Remove clothing
· Wash skin with water or use prepackaged decontamination materials
· Cover all exposed skin and seek medical treatment immediately

In this age of terrorism, if the Secret Service–protected site is suspected of being used by terrorists, the TSD will sweep the location for explosives. Although a training device, this hand grenade was rigged to drop, releasing the pin when the door was opened, and more than likely would have killed everyone in the vicinity. *Henry M. Holden*

"Trust and Confidence," the hallmark of every Secret Service agent, is clear in this photo. In 1910, a Secret Service memorandum titled "Protection for the President," written to the secretary of the Treasury, made clear that the attitude of the Secret Service had remained unaltered—to maintain absolute confidence over their observations of the president: "I wish to say that the men of this service detailed at the presidential home in Washington, or elsewhere, are instructed not to talk of anything they may see or hear. So far as the actions of the president and his family, and social or official callers are concerned, the men are deaf, dumb, and blind. In all the years this service has been maintained at the White House and the freedom with which many important public matters have been discussed in their presence, there has never been a leak or betrayal of trust." As a former director of the Secret Service said before Congress in 1998, "Responsibility in the matter of the safety of the president . . . was accepted willingly when thrust upon us in an emergency and from the beginning has been regarded as a sacred trust, overshadowing in importance all other duties and responsibilities." *Library of Congress*

In 1944, President Franklin D. Roosevelt called for the creation of the Presidential Pilot Office to provide air transportation to the president and his staff. For most of the next twenty years, various four-engine, propeller-driven aircraft were used for presidential air travel. A Douglas C-54 Skymaster nicknamed the Sacred Cow, a four-engine military transport, became the first presidential aircraft, ordered for Franklin D. Roosevelt. The call sign Air Force One was first used in 1959 after confusion arose in flight between an Eastern Airlines flight and the president's plane. From then on, any airplane the president was flying in became known as Air Force One. *U.S. Air Force*

NERVE AGENT CONTAMINATION SIGNS AND SYMPTOMS

- Runny nose
- Pinpoint pupils, dimming vision
- Trouble breathing
- Salivation
- Twitching or convulsions

Craig Miller, a master special officer with the Secret Service, was temporarily assigned to New York in advance of a presidential trip. Miller was the only member of the Secret Service to die on September 11, 2001. He had just completed an overnight shift at the World Trade Center when two hijacked jetliners crashed into the Twin Towers. Miller was helping with rescue work when the towers collapsed. The Secret Service posthumously awarded him the agency's Valor Award, the highest decoration the Secret Service can present.

and coordinate any needed responses with local fire departments and first responders.

All HAMMER team members are selected in a competitive process and receive multidisciplined training to ensure that all team members can perform any of a series of duties. For example, each team member is a certified EMT or paramedic. The skills needed to perform these tasks are perishable, so team members must regularly requalify and receive additional training as technical advancements in their fields take place.

The principal differences between Air Force One and the standard Boeing 747, other than the number of passengers carried, are the electronic and communications equipment, its interior configuration and furnishings, self-contained baggage loader, front and aft air stairs, and the capability for in-flight refueling. These aircraft are flown by the presidential air crew and are assigned to Air Mobility Command's 89th Airlift Wing, Andrews Air Force Base, Maryland. *U.S. Air Force*

The E-4B serves as the National Airborne Operations Center for the president and secretary of defense. In case of national emergency or destruction of ground command and control centers, the aircraft provides a highly survivable command, control, and communications platform to direct U.S. forces, execute emergency war orders, and coordinate actions by civil authorities. *U.S. Air Force*

In 2002, the U.S. Secret Service, in collaboration with the U.S. Department of Education, completed the Safe School Initiative, a study of school shootings and other school-based attacks. The study examined school shootings from 1974 through the end of the school year in 2000, analyzing thirty-seven incidents involving forty-one student attackers. The study found that school shootings are rarely impulsive acts, but are thought out and planned in advance. In addition, prior to most shootings, other kids knew the shooting was to occur, but did not alert an adult. The study also revealed that there is no profile of a school shooter; instead, the students who carried out the attacks differed from one another in numerous ways. However, almost every attacker had engaged in behavior before the shooting that seriously concerned at least one adult. The findings suggested that some school attacks may be preventable. Using the study findings, the Secret Service and Department of Education have modified the Secret Service threat assessment approach for use in schools, to give school and law enforcement professionals tools for investigating threats in school, managing situations of concern, and creating safe school climates.
Henry M. Holden

Protective skills are perishable and require repetition and practice. Here, personnel are designated in different-colored vests to perform specific protective functions around a protectee.

113

SIX

The Secret Service often conducts liaisons with local law enforcement. Here, a Special Agent instructor explains a point. He is flanked by other Secret Service Special Agents and instructors.

Advance Teams and Protection

Several of these Secret Service war wagons, SUV-type vehicles, are part of every motorcade.

The president leaves the safety of the White House several times a week and hundreds of times a year. Advance teams must plan and prepare for these movements outside the White House. "It is important that we have a plan," said one agent. "If you don't have a plan, the game is over before you begin." A critical stage of the protective methodology is the advance team's efforts. Before the protectee's arrival, the lead advance agent holds briefings for all advance team agents and other law enforcement participating in the visit to make sure all are on the same page. The assistance of state, county, and local law enforcement organizations, and sometimes the military, is an essential part of the entire security operation. For security reasons, specific methods of protection and preparation are not revealed; however, there is a great deal of advance planning and coordination in the areas of venue, protection, airspace security, communication, emergency equipment, credentialing, and training. For example, the Secret Service began developing the security plan for the 2004 Democratic National Convention in June 2003. Since the president or other protectee may be making several stops during the trip,

Secret Service agents unload their personal luggage from a 20th Military Airlift Squadron C-141B Starlifter aircraft during Volant Silver, a joint Military Airlift Command and Secret Service operation coordinating vehicle transportation and Secret Service protection for Pope John Paul II when he visited the United States. *Department of Defense*

Secret Service personnel flank the limousine transporting Pope John Paul II from Kelly Air Force Base to San Antonio, one of nine stopping points he made on his visit to the United States. Notice the papal flag on the left fender. *Department of Defense*

During the 2004 Democratic National Convention in Boston, the following agencies were part of the security envelope: U.S. Secret Service; AMTRACK Police; Boston Fire Department; Boston Emergency Management Agency; Boston Emergency Medical Support; Boston Police Department; Bureau of Alcohol, Tobacco, Firearms and Explosives; City of Cambridge Fire Department; City of Cambridge Police Department; Department of Health and Human Services; Department of Defense; Department of Energy; Environmental Protection Agency; Federal Aviation Administration; Federal Bureau of Investigation; Federal Communications Commission; Massachusetts Bay Transportation Authority; Massachusetts Emergency Management Agency; Massachusetts Executive Office of Public Safety; Massachusetts National Guard; Massachusetts State Police; Massachusetts Turnpike Authority; Nuclear Regulatory Commission; U.S. Attorney's Office; U.S. Capitol Police; U.S. Coast Guard; U.S. Food and Drug Administration; U.S. Marshals Service; U.S. Park Police; and U.S. Postal Police.

When an event is designated a national special security event (NSSE), the Secret Service assumes the role of lead agency for the design and implementation of the operational security plan. They are responsible for planning, directing, and executing federal security operations at designated NSSE's. Federal resources, as required, are deployed to maintain the level of security needed for the event and the area. The goal of such an operation is to create a safe environment for all involved—protectees, participants, and the general public. Since September 11, 2001, there have been several national special security events, such as the State of the Union addresses, the Super Bowl, the World Economic Forum in New York, the 2002 Olympics in Utah, the G-8 Summit in Georgia, Democrat and Republican National Conventions, and the 2005 presidential inauguration.

multiple teams of site advance agents and uniformed division personnel are reviewing and enhancing the security at other sites along the travel route.

The Secret Service plans and anticipates every move the president and vice president and others under their protection will make, and tracks these movements at the secret location of the Joint Operations Center (JOC). Outside the White House, there is no margin for error, and the Secret Service never underestimates the adversaries. They know that while they are advancing a site, there may be someone planning to disrupt or compromise a protectee's security.

Uniformed Division personnel are part of the advance teams. The multiple protective rings will start at the event and extend outward, sometimes for miles. Canine teams will respond to bomb threats and suspicious packages, sweep areas to be visited by the protectees, and be on hand for other situations where explosive detection may be necessary.

The Secret Service's responsibility to protect the life of a president is codified in federal statute, Pursuant to Title 18, Section 3056, of the U.S. Code.

A Secret Service agent watches as the Popemobile, visible in the reflection in her sunglasses, is loaded onto a C-5A Galaxy aircraft. *Department of Defense*

TARGETS OF 74 PRINCIPAL INCIDENTS, 1949 TO 1996

Source: Journal of Forensic Sciences
    Secret Service Exceptional Case Study, March 1999

Primary target	Number	Percentage
President	25	34
Other USSS protectees	14	19
Members of Congress	5	7
Federal judges	4	5
State and city officials	2	3
Other national figures	7	10
Business executives	3	4
Entertainment and media celebrities	14	19

Weapon used*	Number	Percentage
Handgun	37	51
Rifle/shotgun	22	30
Knife	11	15
Explosives	6	8
Airplanes	3	4

(* More than one weapon was used in sixteen percent of the incidents.)

The Secret Service learns from attacks on others. On November 30, 1989, Alfred Herrhausen, a key director on the Deutsche Bank board, fell victim to a deadly terrorist bomb shortly after leaving his home in Bad Homberg. He was being chauffeured to work in his armored Mercedes, with bodyguards in both a lead vehicle and another following behind. A light-activated bomb had been hidden in an innocent-looking school bag on a bike next to the road that the terrorists knew Herrhausen would be traveling. In the bag was a forty-four-pound TNT bomb that was detonated when Herrhausen's car interrupted a beam of light as it passed close to the bomb. The bomb and its triggering mechanism were sophisticated, and the bomb targeted the most vulnerable area of Herrhausen's car—the door where he was sitting. It required split-second timing to overcome the car's special armor plating. The terrorists also had to account for the bodyguards' lead vehicle and precisely place the bomb-laden bicycle in such a manner that the blast would do the most damage when it struck the side of Herrhausen's car.

The simulation of a nighttime arrival of a protectee has the trainees on high alert. The civilians in the background are paid role players. A training instructor can be seen coordinating the arrival of a protectee.

Federal law (*posse comitatus*) prohibits military action in domestic affairs without a specific presidential order. *Posse comitatus* (Latin for "power or force of the country") is derived from ancient English law enforcement, which consisted of the shire's force of able-bodied private citizens summoned to assist in maintaining public order. Military antiterrorist groups like the delta force and navy seals are prohibited by this federal law from performing civilian law enforcement duties in the United States or its possessions. However, during high-security events such as a presidential election, the military is called upon to perform security functions.

Secret Service men in black and a member of the armed forces in duty uniforms, with tools of trade in hand, were in attendance for President Clinton's address to the troops in Europe. *Department of Defense*

ADVANCE TEAMS

When the president leaves the safety of the White House, the Secret Service advance teams must make certain that his security remains continuous. Advancing a site will involve hundreds of people, thousands of hours of preparation, and more sophisticated communications and other equipment than most law enforcement agencies possess.

The Secret Service will not discuss protective methods or means in any detail. The advance team surveys each site to minimize the chances of someone with a weapon getting close to any of its protectees. Protective research is an important ingredient in all security operations. The Office of Protective Research (OPR) is responsible for gathering intelligence about threats to protectees. Agents and specialists assigned to protective research also evaluate information received

Deplaning from a U.S. Air Force C-130 Hercules, Secret Service agents and civilian media accompany the secretary of defense at Baghdad International Airport. *Department of Defense*

119

from other law enforcement and intelligence agencies regarding individuals or groups who may pose a threat to protectees. This information is critical to the service's protective planning. "The best way to prevent an assassination attempt," said one agent, "is to have good intelligence and appropriate planning."

The team will review all verbal and written threats made against the protectee(s) from the area and check with local law enforcement for reports of stolen uniforms, and more. From these surveys, the service determines work force, equipment, and other requirements.

Members of the Secret Service and the 2851st Special Police Squadron stand by as Pope John Paul II chats with the crowd following his arrival in Texas.
Department of Defense

In this simulation of a nighttime arrival of a protectee, the Special Agents, in yellow vests, can be seen in a 360-degree circle of protection.

A simulated attack on a protectee has taken place moments earlier, and the trainees have neutralized the threat seen in the background. The protectee can be seen being shoved into the limousine. Two training instructors are carefully watching the trainees repulse the attack. Another is filming the exercise for later debriefing.

Medical emergencies pose one of the highest risks to the president, and all Special Agents on the presidential protective detail (PPD) become experts in "ten-minute medicine." By design, the president is never more than ten minutes away from professional medical attention. Although they do not perform invasive surgery such as a tracheotomy, if it is a heart attack, stroke, or a gunshot wound, agents of the PPD can keep a protectee alive for ten minutes.

VENUE THREATS

At the Democratic and Republican National Conventions in 2004, there were many threat potentials, from subways running under Madison Square Garden in New York City, to catwalks, potted plants that could conceal bombs, and the physical presence of more than forty thousand people in each venue. The Secret Service could not ignore any of them.

The White House Communications Agency (WHCA), originally known as the White House Signal Detachment (WHSD), was officially formed by the War Department on March 25, 1942, during the Roosevelt administration. The detachment was to provide normal and emergency communications requirements in support of the president of the United States. WHSD provided mobile radio, teletype, telephone, and cryptographic aids in the White House and at Shangri-La, now known as Camp David. WHCA provides telecommunications and related support to the president, vice president, White House senior staff, National Security Council, U.S. Secret Service, and others as directed by the White House Military Office.

During the president's various public appearances, such as a slow-moving parade, additional agents dismount and jog or walk alongside the presidential limousine. Their task is to prevent people who may have managed to break through the police cordon from reaching the president's armored vehicle. For distant journeys, Air Force One and several helicopters belonging to the Marine Corps are on round-the-clock standby in a secure area at Andrews Air Force Base.

Secret Service agents and Italian counterterrorist specialists are aboard a security boat on the Grand Canal during the seven-nation economic summit being attended by President Ronald Reagan. *Department of Defense*

To ensure the Democratic presidential nominee's safety at the convention in Boston, parking garages near the convention center were closed and parking was banned on nearby city streets. Officials closed nearby North Station, a major commuter train depot, for the week. Some forty miles of major arteries leading into the city were closed for the four days of the convention from 4 p.m. to 1 a.m.

Secret Service Special Agents and other personnel were posted and alerted to potential specific problems associated with the visit. Intelligence information was evaluated and emergency options outlined. Prior to the arrival of the protectee, the Secret Service established checkpoints and access to the secured area was limited.

A Secret Service driver discusses vehicle-loading operations with an air force senior master sergeant.
Department of Defense

Above: Former President Clinton is flanked by several friends and Secret Service agents on a morning horseback ride. An agent must always be nearby. The only time the president is alone is when an agent is asked to leave a room, and in the private residence. Even there, the agents are just outside the doors. In public, there is at least one agent close enough to cover, pull, or push the president to safety unless the president asks for space, and the Secret Service can overrule him if they feel that would compromise his safety. For example, if the president is giving a commencement speech at a university, at least one of the people in a cap and gown on the stage is an agent. If the president goes horseback riding, as former President Clinton did and President George W. Bush does, the Secret Service spends a lot of time practicing AOPs on horseback. Horses generally do not react well to gunfire or explosions, so it is important to try to predict how they will behave under those conditions.

Every protective agent is identifiable by a small lapel badge. The color and shape of this badge is changed frequently. Wearing this common means of identification is important for the agents in civilian clothes; in the event of an armed attack, the uniformed officers of local law enforcement must be able to tell immediately whether an armed civilian in close proximity to the president is a friend or foe.

Right: Secret Service agents stand watch on a security boat cruising a canal during the seven-nation economic summit being attended by President Ronald Reagan. *Department of Defense*

123

During the visit, the Secret Service command post acted as the nerve center for protective planning and activities, monitoring for emergencies, and keeping the team in contact with one another. Secret Service and local law enforcement personnel working in the command post maintain a communications network of support for members of each protective detail. After the event ends, agents debrief and analyze every step of the protective operation, record unusual incidents, and suggest improvements for the future.

PROTECTIVE DETAIL

Special Agents on the protective details are constantly looking for signs of danger, persons who are acting strangely or unnaturally, and for things that are out of place. Agents on a protective detail are usually seen by the public as anonymous men and women talking into a cuff microphone (on restricted radio channels) and shielded behind dark sunglasses. Special Agents wear sunglasses to keep the sun out of their eyes, which can also increase their ability to see what people in the crowd are doing. If the detail does its job, the rest of the security around the protectee will seem invisible.

The Secret Service seeks to develop combat-ready skills and instant reflexes for use in life-and-death

The Secret Service takes elaborate precautions to prevent attacks. This longtime emphasis on prevention is a hallmark of the Secret Service and stands in contrast to most law enforcement efforts, which strive to catch the criminal after the crime.

Agents on the presidential protection detail (PPD) have one job—protecting the man, the symbol, and the office—and to do this, they must be prepared. Because the skills needed for the PPD are perishable, Special Agents on the protective detail return to the James J. Rowley Training Center every six weeks for two weeks of refresher training.

In the past, agents have dressed as major league umpires, soldiers, engineers, academics, and priests, in an effort to achieve seamless proximity to a protectee regardless of the context.

Former President and Mrs. Clinton are flanked by Secret Service agents at a state dinner in China.

A parade limousine at the 2001 presidential inauguration. The license plate "USA 2" indicates it is the vice president's limousine. That plate is only used during inauguration ceremonies. All other times the parade limousines carry generic Washington, D.C., plates.

A coast guard petty officer looks over New York City during security preparations for the Republican National Convention in August 2004. The U.S. Coast Guard was part of the team providing security during the convention. The 2004 campaign saw unprecedented levels of security. U.S. Coast Guard

The inauguration parade of President George W. Bush saw the heaviest security of any inauguration. The Secret Service is responsible for the security but calls upon local and other law enforcement and the military to augment security. *Department of Defense*

President George H. W. Bush arrives by limousine at Naval Air Station (NAS) Miramar. It appears that all the personnel in the photo are Secret Service agents. *Department of Defense*

Air Force One is at Hickam Air Force Base with President George W. Bush on board for his first visit to Hawaii while holding office. In the background is an identical VC-25 setting up to land. *Department of Defense*

First Lady Laura Bush reads a story to youngsters at the annual Easter egg roll at the White House. The Secret Service makes a limited background check on everyone who is admitted to the White House beyond the normal White House tour.

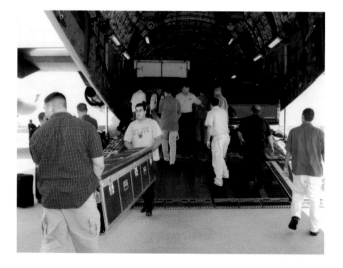

Everything needed to support the president outside the White House, from the countersniper teams, Emergency Response Teams, communications gear, and more, is flown in one or more Air Force Lockheed C-5A Galaxy or other aircraft.

situations, such as an assassination attempt on a protectee. Special Agents who have made it to the PPD have been described as being not just type-A personalities but type-A squared. They are individuals who are under control of their emotions during times of stress; smart, meticulous planners; and are prepared to step up when the time comes. They are not the biggest or the strongest, but rather the swiftest and the smartest.

An attack can happen in milliseconds, and agents must be ready. Special Agents prepare for this by training regularly to cover and relocate a protectee, and react within a split second to an incident. Agents train to respond to any sound, such as gunfire. On the protective detail, agents are focused and expecting the unexpected. It can be stressful. One agent described the feeling as similar to "being inside a jack-in-the-box, waiting to spring into action."

On March 30, 1981, President Ronald Reagan was leaving a Washington hotel after delivering a speech. Shots rang out. Special Agent Tim McCarthy sprang into action and jumped in front of the president, taking a bullet in the stomach. Also wounded were two police officers and the president's press secretary, James Brady. Two other Secret Service agents grabbed the president, pushed him safely inside his armored limousine, and sped away. On the

The crowd of several hundred thousand saw President George W. Bush take the oath of office and watched the 2005 inaugural parade. They had to enter one by one through twenty-two airline-style security checkpoints. Aerosol cans, backpacks, and any bags over eight inches wide were prohibited. Federal agents, some of them in plain clothes, patrolled within the crowd with pocket-sized sensors to check for toxins and radiation. Major streets were closed to vehicles for more than a day, and black-uniformed Secret Service countersnipers were posted atop buildings for the most extensively guarded inauguration in presidential history. On the ground, measures included high-tech mobile command offices to communicate with the thousands of security officials and check out reports of potential trouble. A lower-tech part of the effort deployed teams with bomb-sniffing dogs to inspect buildings, garages, and delivery trucks. The day's events were captured on fourteen fixed television cameras that transmitted views to a monitoring center in nearby suburban Virginia. The glass partition seen in the photo is ballistic protection for the president.

As late as the 1976 presidential campaign, the public had almost intimate access to the president. President Gerald Ford is on his way to the Republican National Convention in an open-topped limousine, with Secret Service agents in obvious numbers close to him. *Library of Congress*

way back to the White House, SAIC Jerry Parr patted the president down, looking for a wound. He did not find one. However, when the president wiped some bright red, foamy blood from his mouth with a handkerchief, Parr knew from his training that the president had been shot in a vital area, either in or near the lungs. The president's wound was from a small-caliber gun and not a direct hit from the shooter's gun, but a ricochet off the limousine's door. Parr redirected the driver to Georgetown Hospital just three minutes away. This quick thinking, developed through years of training, likely saved the president's life.

The two police officers and Special Agent McCarthy, who was willing to give his life for the president, recovered from their wounds. James Brady also recovered but was severely disabled from a head wound.

"Agent McCarthy put his body in the line of fire, between President Reagan and the gunman," said Parr. "That gave me time to get the president into the vehicle. I owe my life to him. He did what he was trained to do. He put his body in front of the president."

As a young boy, SAIC Parr had seen a movie about the Secret Service. He was so impressed with the character Special Agent Brass Bancroft that he told his father when he grew up he wanted to be a Secret Service agent. In the movie, Ronald Reagan played the character of Brass Bancroft.

An airman from the 100th Security Forces Squadron, RAF Mildenhall, provides security for part of the U.S. presidential support team aircraft during a refueling stop in June 2003. *U.S. Air Force*

While the president may appear to be alone and move about freely when he approaches Marine One, Secret Service agents are just off camera. Countersnipers are on rooftops, and ERT are in the bushes, behind trees, and elsewhere. Uniformed officers are highly visible and at all access points. It is reasonable to assume that any of the presidential white-top helicopters probably have a wide range of countermeasures against potential threats; the details are, for obvious reasons, classified. However, an aviation buff would notice several blisters, bulges, and antennae. The interiors of these aircraft are also off-limits to the public and shielded by heavily tinted, perhaps armored, Plexiglas. President Dwight D. Eisenhower was the first president to travel aboard a helicopter, a Sikorsky UH-34. The helicopter was not air conditioned, so the marines painted the top of the fuselage white, to reflect sunlight and help cool the interior. The tradition has lasted since 1957. At least one presidential helicopter, designated Marine One, travels with the president and is ready to fly him to a hospital if he has a medical emergency. Often the president travels with dozens of aircraft. When President Clinton traveled to India in March 2000, seventy-six U.S. Air Force airplanes went with him. *Henry M. Holden*

THE SIXTH SENSE

Training and constant skills reviews are the hallmarks of a successful agent. While sounding like science fiction, the sixth sense is more than just training; it is listening to one's instincts, honed through training, and being on the job. It is a "visceral feeling."

Former Special Agent Rufus Youngblood, who dove on top of Vice President Lyndon Johnson when shots rang out in Dallas on November 22, 1963, described it this way: "You are constantly on the alert for the individual who somehow does not fit. You scan the crowd, the rooftops,

Secret Service agents hold back the crowd trying to see President Lyndon Johnson and Ladybird Johnson, the first lady, at one of the inaugural balls. To the left and behind Ladybird is Vice President Hubert H. Humphrey. Today, the Secret Service would not allow this close-in push of the crowd to happen. *Library of Congress*

The president is constantly under the eyes of the Secret Service, no matter where he travels. President William J. Clinton is walking on the Brooklyn, New York, shore with only Secret Service agents present.

Only Marine One can take off and land at the White House. Not even the vice president's Marine Two can land there. Although it appears that Marine One may fly alone, there are generally other helicopters that fly with the president. These helicopters usually contain White House staff, the press, and Secret Service, and the helicopters fly out of a nearby air base and rendezvous with Marine One in the air. The idea, presumably, is to play a shell game with any potential aerial threat. The more helicopters in the air, the more of a challenge it is to figure out which one has POTUS. Pilots of the classified white-topped helicopters must have a top-secret SCI Yankee White security clearance. Yankee White is a security clearance compartment associated with White House presidential support duties. *Henry M. Holden*

His Excellency, President Hamid Karzai, of Afghanistan, was under the protection of the U.S. Secret Service on his visit to the United States.

the doorways, and the windows, ready to take whatever action necessary."

Today, all people in a crowd close to the president are screened by Uniformed Division officers through magnetometers. However, the Secret Service is never dependent on machinery or technology alone to guard its protectees. Special Agents stand ready by combining their perception with intensive training to the point where they do not have to think about what to do but react automatically to a threat. They endlessly repeat hundreds of maneuvers to create a Pavlov-like response. "It is muscle memory," said one agent. They do not stop to think about

it and then make a decision. It is a reaction resulting from repetitive training.

Reacting instantly, a sign of excellent training, has saved more than one president's life. Agent Larry Buendorf was on President Ford's detail and standing immediately to his left as the president shook hands in Sacramento, California, on September 5, 1975. He had, a moment before, noticed a young woman in a bright red dress mirroring the president's movements: that is, moving along as the president moved along the crowd. "All of a sudden I see a hand coming up, very slowly, with an object in it," said Buendorf. Without thinking, Buendorf stepped

Special Agent Nick Zarvos was shot in the throat in the attempted assassination of presidential candidate Governor George Wallace. Zarvos survived, as did Governor Wallace, who was wounded and partially paralyzed.

On 9/11, the Secret Service put the Continuity of Government Plan into action. They had to locate all those in the line of presidential succession and provide protection to the president, the vice president, and others next in order of succession to the office of the president: speaker of the House of Representatives, president pro tempore of the Senate, secretary of state, and their families.

Following the president are Deputy White House Chief of Staff Karl Rove and Assistant to the President and Deputy Chief of Staff Harriet Miers. Scott McClellan, the president's press secretary, is on the far right. While the president's staff members are the only people seen with him in this photo, countersnipers and Emergency Response Team members are present but well hidden. The fire engine, also generally off camera, is a precaution taken because the president is about to board Marine One. *Henry M. Holden*

A launch carrying President George H. W. Bush makes its way through the Upper New York Bay flanked by coast guard, local and state police, and Secret Service escorts. Wherever a president goes, security is the foremost concern. The Verrazano Narrows Bridge is in the background. *U.S. Coast Guard*

in front of the president and grabbed the object. "The minute I did that, I knew it was a gun," he said. Buendorf pulled the gun from her hand, and pushed her away from the president. Buendorf was in the right place, at the right time, and his instincts saved the president. The rest of the team did exactly what they were trained to do: they covered the president and relocated him. Agents understand on an instinctive level that there is no time to think about losing. "On the PPD, every day is Super Bowl Sunday," said one agent. "We can't afford to lose today, because we can't catch up tomorrow. This is what we are trained to do. The moves become automatic."

Because the job of Secret Service agent is physically demanding, agents must maintain their strength and stamina throughout their careers. The Secret Service requires that agents engage in frequent and regular exercise. Special Agents are tested quarterly to assess their physical fitness. They are tested in five areas: pushups, situps, pull-ups, a 1.5-mile run, and the sit-and-reach flexibility test. Their responsibility is to guard the president and first family, and provide escape and communications in the event of a paramilitary attack on the White House. Agents must be in excellent condition to carry, if necessary, the president and members of the first family through a prearranged escape route.

The gaping maw of a C-5A Galaxy shows a parade limousine being removed. Generally there are at least two limousines in any motorcade; one is a decoy to halve the chances of a successful AOP. The Secret Service uses a variety of heavy-lift airplanes such as the C-5, C-17, and, until its recent retirement, the C-141 Globemaster.

Agents of a protective detail will often appear with their coats or jackets open so that, if necessary, they can easily draw their weapons. The flag on this limousine indicates there likely is a visiting British dignitary inside.

The Easter Bunny cannot hop the fence to get to the Easter egg roll. He has to pass the Secret Service security screening like everyone else.

PERIMETERS

The security of the president always extends outward from him. The Secret Service began using the concentric circle formations after World War II. It was derived from football, where the ball carrier advances forward toward the goal line, protected by his teammates, who intercept any opposition players who try to tackle him. Substitute the ball for the president or protectee, the ball carrier for the protectee's personal agent, and the fielders or outer ring of the protective detail for the Special Agents. The concept is simple and now used by most governments. The protectee's personal agent covers and relocates him. The outer perimeter of agents moves against the threat.

continued on page 137

President George W. Bush, flanked by two Secret Service agents, descends the stairs of Air Force One after arriving at Lajes Field, Azores, for a one-day emergency summit meeting. *Department of Defense*

Major presidential and vice presidential candidates and their spouses receive protection beginning 120 days before a general presidential election.
Presidents Abraham Lincoln, James Garfield, William McKinley, and John F. Kennedy were all fatally wounded by assassins. As a result of the Kennedy assassination, Secret Service protection was extended to former presidents and their families. In 1997, Congressional legislation limited Secret Service protection of former presidents for a period of not more than ten years from the date the former president leaves office. The legislation also provided Secret Service protection for children of former presidents until age sixteen and for visiting heads of foreign states or governments and their spouses traveling with them, other distinguished foreign visitors, and official representatives of the United States performing special missions abroad.

Agents on any protective detail are usually seen as anonymous men and women talking into cuff microphones and shielded behind dark sunglasses. It is clear from this photo taken with the Brooklyn Bridge in the background that the Secret Service never drops its guard.

A transportation advance agent is on the radio coordinating plans for the president's visit. Barely seen is the handheld microphone and earpiece in her right ear. Agents communicate over a restricted radio network impervious to eavesdropping. With this network, every agent knows where the president is at all times.

A mechanic/driver and two Special Agents listen as the transportation advance agent briefs the team.

According to a *New York Times* report, in the 1993 World Trade Center bombing, an armored Secret Service limousine was parked about one hundred feet from a truck bomb. Although the bomb blast crashed through five stories of concrete and the concussion destroyed cars all over the floor where the limousine was parked, the Secret Service limousine "did not even have a broken windshield," according to a government official on the scene that day.

Since the 1970s, when the president travels out of Washington, D.C., generally his motorcade varies in size. Each vehicle may contain counterassault teams, intelligence teams that keep track of threats, and an undisclosed number and type of weapons systems. The vice-presidential motorcade generally consists of a similar arrangement. *Department of Defense*

AIR INCURSIONS

One would think the methods of actual and attempted assassinations of a U.S. president would be varied, but in fact, the only successful method has been the firearm. Not only has no other device or technique ever been successful, but also to the best of public knowledge, there has only been one other method attempted—using an aircraft. The few attempts in small airplanes all failed.

The presidential motorcade progresses down Pennsylvania Avenue, taking the president and the first lady to the White House. The presidential limousine is the embodiment of the "presidential bubble." Secret Service members on both sides of the car provide a 360-degree circle of protection during the presidential inaugural parade. When the bulletproof presidential bubble moves, everything moves out of its way. Notice the ceremonial license plate number "1" signifying the president is aboard. *Department of Defense*

Former President Clinton was the last president entitled to lifetime Secret Service protection after he left office. All future presidents will receive ten years of protection once they leave office.

The massive interior of the U.S. Air Force C-5A Galaxy will carry at least two parade limousines, an SUV, a truck, and dozens of Secret Service personnel. These cars fly in pairs on cargo planes in advance of any presidential trip.

President George W. Bush and First Lady Laura Bush enjoy their first inaugural parade. While all presidents wish to be close to the public, walks of this type are kept at a minimum. Note the Secret Service agents are close enough to the couple to react instantly to protect them.

RADIO CODE NAMES

To maintain secrecy in radio communications, primary protectees receive code names. All presidents are called POTUS (president of the United States), but are also assigned personalized code names, picked by the military. Sometimes these names reflect an idiosyncrasy of the individual. President Ronald Reagan, a former cowboy actor who frequently vacationed on his ranch in California, was called Rawhide, and his ranch was called Brimstone. George H. W. Bush was Timberwolf, Sheepskin, and Snowstorm. Richard Nixon was Searchlight. President George W. Bush has had the names Tumbler and Trailblazer. (Once the media knows a name, it is changed.) President Jimmy Carter was Dasher and Deacon. President Bill Clinton was called Eagle, while his vice president, Al Gore, famous for his wooden speaking style, got the name Sawhorse. Dan Quayle, vice president under President George H. W. Bush, was called Scorecard because of his fondness for golf. Rumor spread that Clinton's accident-prone brother Roger was code-named Headache. In fact, Roger Clinton was not a Secret Service protectee. Everyone in the presidential family also gets a code name. The first lady is called FLOTUS (first lady of the United States), and she also gets a personalized name. Hillary Clinton was Evergreen, her daughter Chelsea was Energy, Nancy Reagan was Rainbow, Pat Nixon was Starlight, Barbara Bush was Tranquility, and Laura Bush was Tempo.

One reason for the Secret Service's success is its agents' skills in working with other agencies. Moving the president is an enormous challenge, requiring close cooperation between the military, White House staff, state and local police, and the Secret Service. It is the "interagency coordination" that makes every move successful.

continued from page 132
CONCLUSION

The Secret Service is built on the extraordinary efforts of people in the past. Their patriotism, professionalism, and dedication to duty call out to those now in the Secret Service to maintain those high standards.

Today's Secret Service personnel are an ordinary group of people doing an extraordinary job, an honor few

As of 2004, the Secret Service has lost 35 employees to on-duty incidents, six of whom died in the April 19, 1995, terrorist bombing of the Alfred P. Murrah Federal Building in Oklahoma City. The last agent died in a traffic accident on his way back to his field office. Fortunately, very few agents and officers have been shot while guarding the president or other protectees, but the risks are always there. Examples of employees who have been shot are Special Agent Nick Zarvos, Uniformed Officer Leslie Coffelt, and Special Agent Tim McCarthy. Officer Coffelt was shot and killed in 1950 when two Puerto Rican nationalists tried to assassinate President Harry Truman. On November 1, 1950, President Harry Truman was living in Blair House while the White House was being remodeled. White House police officer Floyd Boring was on duty that day, standing guard at the front door. "The president was upstairs," Boring said, "having a nap before he was due to go to Arlington to lay a wreath." Boring and other uniformed officers were outside on the steps when two men approached. One pulled out a gun and aimed it at Boring. "I heard it snap, and I pulled out my gun and shot back. Then everybody was shooting." Officer Coffelt fell mortally wounded, but first he shot and killed one of the men. It was all over in twenty seconds. "I realized later that the man aiming at me had forgotten to cock his Lugar pistol," said Boring. "Mr. Truman was never in any real danger. He was to leave by the back door, and they wouldn't have a chance at him." Two other guards, Donald T. Birdzell and Joseph H. Downs, were shot, but both recovered. The forty-year-old Coffelt died that evening. After three previous cold-blooded presidential assassinations and several failed attempts against President Truman, Congress enacted legislation that permanently authorized Secret Service protection of the president and his immediate family.

Above: The presidential limousine is obviously longer than a regular Cadillac limousine. Since the president is never out of touch, the added piece in the midsection may hold communications gear. Note the presidential seal on the rear door. Cadillac limousines have long served the White House. President Woodrow Wilson was the first president to ride in a Cadillac, during the World War I victory parade. Later presidents used a 1928 Cadillac until 1938, when two Cadillac convertibles nicknamed the Queen Mary and Queen Elizabeth replaced it. The two 7,660-pound vehicles were equipped with two-way radios and heavy-duty generators. The two Queens served Presidents Roosevelt, Truman, and Eisenhower. In 1956, the Queen Mary II and Queen Elizabeth II convertibles replaced the original series. The new vehicles were twenty-one feet long and weighed 7,000 pounds. Like their predecessors, these fully armored vehicles had state-of-the art communications at that time, and were fitted with narrow rims inside the tire in case the tires were shot out. The Queen Mary II and Queen Elizabeth II served Presidents Eisenhower, Kennedy, and Johnson. Both vehicles were retired in 1968. The Reagan administration used a 1983 Cadillac Fleetwood limousine, and the Clinton administration used a Cadillac Fleetwood Brougham. The predecessor to the current limousine was the 2001 Cadillac DeVille limousine used by President George H. W. Bush. The parade limousine, or presidential vehicle, is the pride of the Secret Service fleet. It is a highly modified 2006 General Motors Cadillac DTS Presidential Limousine, whose weight and cost is classified. In addition to their use for Secret Service driver training, retired cars from the White House fleet are sent to U.S. government stations around the nation and the world for use by ambassadors, other VIPs, and dignitaries.

When the president travels in the vehicle, presidential seals are affixed to the exterior rear doors. A U.S. flag is mounted on the right front fender, and the presidential standard is on the left front fender. Flush-mounted, high-intensity discharge spotlights illuminate the flags at night.

On February 8, 2001, a middle-aged accountant with a history of mental illness fired five shots just outside the White House fence at the edge of the South Lawn, a few hundred yards from the building where President George W. Bush was inside exercising. The gunfire sent tourists running for cover. Secret Service officers on patrol in a car "heard shots fired" over their radio, and proceeded to surround a subject who was wielding a gun. During the ten-minute standoff, witnesses said they heard officers try to persuade the man to put the gun down. When he raised the gun again and started aiming it at people, a member of the Secret Service's Emergency Response Team shot him in the right leg.

To the U.S. Secret Service, presidents and other protectees can sometimes be a tough challenge. The Secret Service agents must go where the protectee goes, from skydiving to water and snow environments.

In November 1963, President John F. Kennedy was assassinated in Dallas, Texas. Lee Harvey Oswald was arrested for the crime. At the time, it was not a federal crime to murder the president, so neither the FBI nor the Secret Service could take Oswald into custody. Oswald was taken to the Dallas county jail, where, because of inadequate security arrangements, he was shot dead before he could be tried for the crime.

Americans attain. September 11, 2001, redefined and increased the stress level for the personnel. They believe in what they do and know why they are doing it. Many were on duty on 9/11, and had to swallow their horror and do their job. Most look at what they do not as a job but a way of life; it's about doing the right thing. They mark a good day when nothing bad has happened to any of their protectees.

The Secret Service studies past assassinations and attempted assassinations worldwide to see what caused the security breach. They will run the videotapes or film repeatedly until they determine what happened and how, and if, it can be prevented in the future.

It was clear from the John F. Kennedy assassination that the removable top on the limousine was no longer an option, and more agents on, near, and in the car might have made a difference. According to former Secret Service Director Lewis Merletti, "An analysis of the ensuing assassination (including the trajectory of the bullets which struck the president) indicates that it might have been thwarted had agents been stationed on the car's running boards. In other words, had they been able to maintain close proximity to the president during the motorcade, the assassination of John F. Kennedy might have been averted." After the assassination of President Kennedy, the Secret Service had the presidential limousine's armor plating reinforced.

Until Robert F. Kennedy's assassination shortly after winning the California primary in 1968, presidential candidates lived outside the protective bubble of the Secret Service. His assassination illustrated the need for an official protective detail, not a private bodyguard as Kennedy had, for presidential candidates. After that assassination, presidential candidates became Secret Service protectees in the 120 days before the election.

Four years later, the attempted assassination of Alabama's governor George Wallace, which wounded Special Agent Nick Zarvos, illustrated that magnetometers at crowds are necessary for protecting presidential candidates. In the handgun attacks on the president and candidates, if magnetometers had been available, they would have detected the weapon and the individual would have been detained.

From 1998 to 2003, as al Qaeda ramped up its war against the United States, the Secret Service's roster of agents grew by forty percent; its budget jumped by eighty percent.

Ground clearance is tight, and air force personnel and Special Agents carefully back down one of the parade limousines. At some venues, the Secret Service will produce several decoy presidential limousines. When President Clinton visited Pakistan in 2000, there were six presidential limousines, which would give any potential terrorist attack only a one-in-six chance of success if they struck only one of the vehicles.

These Secret Service agents are looking at hands and faces. People on a rope line should be smiling, happy, and pleased to get close to the president. If someone is not smiling or has a blank look on his face, one of the agents will alert the undercover agents who are in the crowd and close to the rope line. They will not confront such an individual unless he makes a threatening move.

Appendix A

HONOR ROLL
Secret Service Personnel Killed in On-Duty Incidents

Operative William Craig	1902
Operative Joseph A. Walker	1907
Operative Robert K. Webster	1927
Operative James W. Hair	1928
Operative Robert L. Godby	1935
Special Agent James A. Hollinger	1936
Special Agent Henry E. Thomas	1936
Special Agent August A. Gennerich	1936
Special Agent Thomas E. Vaughan	1940
Officer Leslie J. Coffelt	1950
Special Agent Thomas B. Shipman	1963
Special Agent Thomas K. Wooge	1968
Special Agent J. Clifford Dietrich	1973
Special Agent James M. Ryan	1977
Special Agent Perry S. Watkins	1980
Special Agent Julie Y. Cross	1980
Special Agent Donald A. Bejcek	1983
Special Agent George P. LaBarge	1983
Special Agent Donald W. Robinson	1983
Special Agent Richard T. Cleary	1986
Special Agent Manuel de J. Marrero-Otero	1986
Special Agent Marvin E. Gilpin	1989
Special Agent James Steven Collins	1992
Special Agent Cynthia L. Brown	*1995
Special Agent Donald R. Leonard	*1995
Special Agent Mickey B. Maroney	*1995
Office Manager Linda G. McKinney	*1995
Investigative Assistant Kathy L. Seidl	*1995
Special Agent Allan G. Whicher	*1995
Protective Support Technician Aldo E. Frascoia	1996
Special Agent Daniel M. Connolly	1996
Special Agent Hector L. Diaz	1997
Special Agent Scott E. Deaton	1999
Master Special Officer Craig Miller	2001
Special Agent Phillip Lebid	2004

* Died in the bombing of the Alfred P. Murrah Federal Building in Oklahoma City, Oklahoma

Appendix B

ACRONYMS AND DEFINITIONS

Acronyms:

AFIS—Automated Fingerprint Identification System
AOP—attack on the principal (anyone under the protection of the Secret Service)
ASAIC—assistant Special Agent in charge
BFO—Beltsville field office
BICE—Bureau of Immigration and Customs Enforcement
CAT—counterassault team
CERT—computer emergency readiness team
CID—Criminal Investigative Division
CITP—Criminal Investigator Training Program
DODPI—Department of Defense Polygraph Institute
ECTF—Electronic Crimes Task Force
EMT—emergency medical technician
ERT—Emergency Response Team
FISH—Forensic Information System for Handwriting
FLETC—Federal Law Enforcement Training Center
FLOTUS —first lady of the United States
FO—field office
FSD—Forensic Services Division
HAMMER—Hazardous Agent Mitigation Medical Emergency Response
JOC—Joint Operations Center
KSA—knowledge, skills, and abilities (test)
LEO—law enforcement officer
NTAC—National Threat Assessment Center
NSSE—national special security event
OJT—on-the-job training
POTUS—president of the United States
PPD—presidential protective detail
PSS—physical security specialists
RA—resident agency
RO—resident office
SAIC —Special Agent in charge: a field office supervisor
SOT—special operations team
TEA—treasury enforcement agent (exam)
TSD—Technical Security Division
UC—undercover
WHCA—White House Communications Agency

Definitions:

Acrophobia—fear of heights
Fidelity—loyalty, faithfulness
Frangible bullets—lead-free bullets that are 100 percent safe when hitting anything as hard as or harder than the bullet. A frangible bullet turns to dust when it hits something hard, and it shoots just as well as plated bullets.
Indictment—a formal accusation of wrongdoing, usually issued by a grand jury. An individual charged by indictment is presumed innocent until proven guilty at some later criminal proceedings.
Integrity—honesty and uprightness
Money laundering—the process by which proceeds from a criminal activity are disguised to conceal their illicit origins
On the job—generic expression for an active-duty law enforcement officer.
Posse Comitatus—a force of able-bodied private citizens summoned to assist in maintaining public order.
Racketeer Influenced and Corrupt Organization (RICO) Statute—a federal statute designed to combat the infiltration of racketeers and organized crime into legal organizations engaged in interstate commerce. The statute also applies to individuals, businesses, political protest groups, and terrorist organizations.
Release the crime scene—allow it to be opened for cleanup or to public access
Squad—a team of Special Agents dedicated to one enforcement discipline (i.e. cyber crime)
Statute of limitations—a time limit during which a crime can be prosecuted. In the United States only three crimes are unbound by any statute of limitation: homicide, tax evasion, and espionage.
Stove piping—the vertical integration of an organization where there is no cross communication
Street agent—an agent removed from the policy and administrative decision-making processes
Walk-in—a volunteer who walks into an embassy or consulate and offers his or her services as a spy

Index

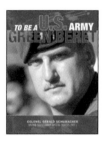

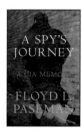

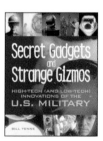